International Friendship
The Gifts from Africa

CHE ONEJOON

KEHRER

A note on the romanization of names:
For the names of North and South Korean historical figures whose names are already known in the English language, the most common or widely used spellings of their name has been used (e.g. Kim Il Sung, Park Chung-hee). The names of the individual authors of each paper have been spelled according to their preferred spellings, where known. In the case of all other names, the official romanization system in North Korea has been employed.

CONTENTS

Dr. Sam Nujoma founding
president and father of the
Namibian nation

AMA II   SEBELE I   BATHOEN I

75

KHAMA III

Joshua Nkomo
Former Vice-President of Zimbabwe

This is not a national army. Let's make it plain here. It is the 5th Brigade, and the 5th Brigade saves itself. It is not a government organ. It is a party organ. But this killing field I couldn't possibly keep quiet, couldn't possibly. So I can't stand by that.

Michael Sibangilizwe Nkomo
Joshua Nkomo's Son

When I heard that it was a North Korean statue, I was devastated. I didn't imagine that our own people, our own government, could once more engage the North Koreans to do something like that. If they really wanted to honor my father that way, I think a Zimbabwean could've done that. There is a lot of artists here in Zimbabwe that could've easily done that for us. If we can't do it, there are friends in neighboring countries who can do that for us. Of all the people, North Koreans, I don't think they are qualified, at all, to construct a statue for us. I think that's an insult more than anything.

Built by North Korean in Bulawayo city centre
in Auguest 2010 and Removed in September 2010

TCR 10:23.32.29

5여단이 말하거를 자신들은
자발적으로 움직인다고 했습니다.

TCR 10:32.39.12

1.AUTHENTICITY
2.HONESTY
3.TRANSPARENCY
4.ACCOUNTABILITY
5.INTEGRITY
6.COMMITMENT

만약 우리가 제작을 못하게 된다 하면, 이웃 나라의
친구들이 우리를 위해 제작을 해줄 수 있었습니다.

Larger-than-life statue Specialist h
ogy dedicated to open next
iMdala wethu
abuko Nkomo

of the country

TCR 10:25.37.28

in training and equipping his
private army the Fifth brigade.

TCR 10:24.29.10

짐바브웨 아프리칸 인민연

당신은 그 공격을
그의 동상을 만들었다

APU 정당의 리더입니다

바로 그 사람들이
상상할 수 있습니까?

Great Zimbabwe
UNESCO Worl...
Masvingo P...

조선 민주주의
D. P. I
동상 젯푸...

우리가 주로 걱정한
영웅들만을

우리는 영웅에
조각가들의 건...

ional Monument
itage Centre
e, Zimbabwe

인민 공화국
OF. KOREA,
1982 8 1 거림

영웅릉은 국가적인
이기 때문에

시 WORK예술가와
서 있었기 때문에

IWE NENI TINE BASA

THE NATIONAL HEROES ACRE

Mrs. Doreen Sibanda
Director of the National Gallery of Zimbabwe

We were aware of the controversy when it (the statue) was built because there was a lot of outcry from local artists and local sculptors. Particularly, (I am) thinking that would be an opportunity for them to show their prowess. However, the sculpture was created by North Korean artists. And it's withstood the test of time considerably. It's very heroic. I think obviously that this is the strong tradition of creating this type of heroic and socialist realism work. And in that sense, it's very appropriate.

Paul Bakua-Lufu Badibanga
Deputy Director of the National Museum of Kinshasa

Even though ordinary people criticize the monuments built by the Koreans, I would take the example of the Lumumba statue at the entrance to Kinshasa. We see that we presented Lumumba overweight and with a belly. However, Lumumba did not have a large belly. So the image of the Lumumba statue does not present Lumumba as he was. There are also criticisms about the statue of President Kasavubu. So I would say without being an expert that even ordinary people criticize the way these statues are present. Ordinary people even do not understand the change of material. We know that when tin or zinc is exposed to the sun, it will discolor and so on. But I have heard people say that the statue of Kasavubu that was erected not long ago is quickly fading.

The Statues of The se
El Hadj Oma

Built in

이 동상은 가봉인들에게는
혁신적인 것이었습니다.

It
innovativ

그런 점에서 아름다운 이야기인 것입니다.

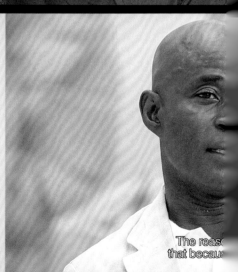

The reas
that becaus

d President of Gabon
ngo Ondimba

rly 80s, 90s

Joseon(Kingdom)–Pyongyang
춘선–평양

abonese.

Christian Ndong
Menzamet

Sculptor, Painter

say so is
odyssey.

Pierre Goudiaby Atepa
Senegalese Architect

Big bronze sculptures. Only north Koreans know how to do it. They are the best—no question about it. The phase of the design is very simple. You first had the original idea. And the will of doing it came from the former president. I was his special advisor, and I was his architect. So he called me and said, "Pierre, you know the book that I wrote 30 years back. I was imagining coming out of the mountain, a couple of Africans, one African, his wife, and his child coming out of the mountain and pointing. So can you make a design for me?" So I did the design, and then I called my Korean friends. We made a lot of sketches, and we decided that this was a good one. We studied together with the structure, of course, how to build it here in Senegal, how to bring the bronze sheets, mold them, etc. It took about a year and a half, but it was very good. We'll show you the pictures, of course, of the process, you know, piece by piece. Pieces were about 1.5 to 2 meters, square meters, piece by piece by piece. And as you know, the monument took about 200 tons of bronze. The man is about 100 tons, the lady is about 75 tons, and the kid is 25 tons.

Of course, S
have made

The sta
were ha

Korea should
necessity.

/ store
g here.

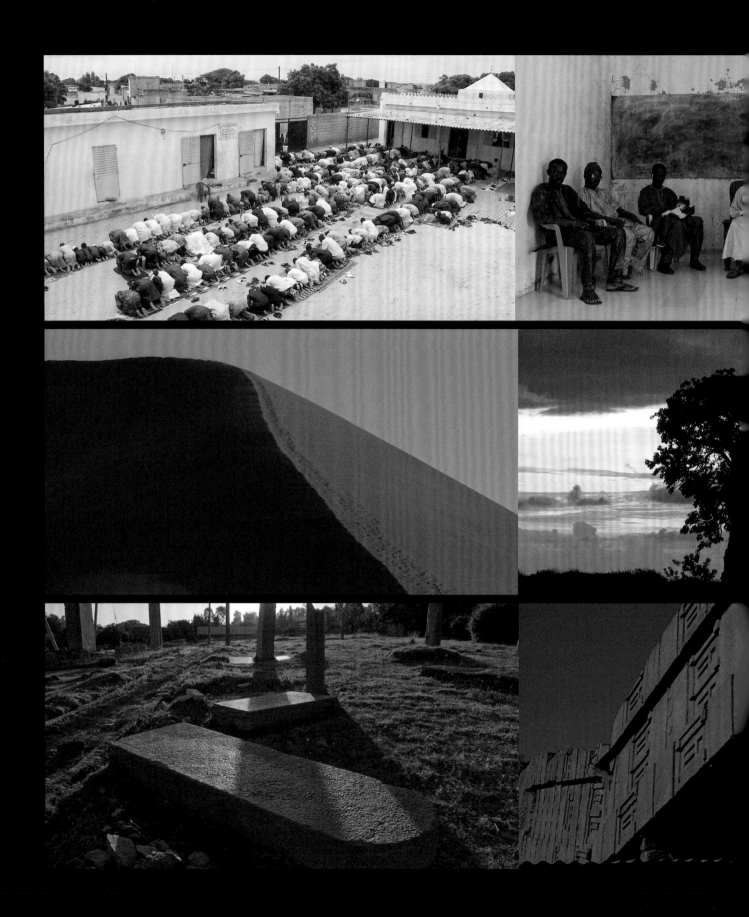

우리는 《유엔군사령부》의 해체와 남조선으로부터의 모든 외국군대의 철거를 요구한다

보쯔와나대표의 연설

【유엔본부 11월 1일 조선중앙통신 특파원발】10월 28일 유엔총회 제1위원회에서 보쯔와나대표 모카미가 연설하였다.

그의 연설은 다음과 같다.

토론이 거의 끝날무렵 22년이 지났다. 조선인민의 의사에 배치되게 조선은 아직도 분렬되여있다. 나는 우리 나라의 평화통일을 이룩하려는 조선인민의 숙망에 큰 동정심을 가지고 따라보았다는 것을 강조하는바이다.

우리 대표단은 1972년 7월 4일의 남북공동성명에 표명된 원칙에 따라 통일을 이룩하려는

조선인민의 념원을 전폭적으로 공동한다. 우리 대표단은 1973년 ...위원회에서 보쯔와나대표 모카미가 연설하였다.

우리 대표단은 조선인민이 자신의 문제를 결정할 자유를 갖도록 하기 위하여 남조선으로부터 모든 외국군대를 철거시켜야 한다고 믿는다. 그럼으로 우리는 《유엔군사령부》의 해체와 남조선으로부터의 모든 외국군대의 철거를 요구한다.

우리는 또한 이미 22년이나 존재하고있는 정전협정이 아직 조선의 항구적평화를 위한 조치에로 나아가야 한다고 믿는다. 사실 일시적인 조치일뿐 한 민족이 무한히 살것을 기대하는것은

공정하지 못하였다. 유엔은 긴 남조선에서 항구적인 평화를 이룩하는 데 기여하여야 한다.

또한 우리 대표단의 견해로는 《유엔군사령부》의 해체와 모든 외국군대의 철거 그리고 조선에 있던 시킬 수 ...외국군대를 계속 주문시킬 필요성을 제거하려는 남아있는 요소를 제거하는것이다.

우리는 또한 조선의 두 부분의 평화적의사의 표시로서 쌍방의 무력을 줄일데 대한 원칙을 지지한다. 우리는 이것이 정전협정에서 군비경쟁과 긴장상태를 완화시켜 조선반도에서 전정한 평화를 ...철정이라고 믿는다.

우리 대표단은 에이 ... 1—엽 709결의안을 지지한다.

우리는 키프러스 ...프리카의 평화 경제문제 문화문제에 기여하게될 건설과...는 태양적인 조직을 취하여야 한다. 《유엔군사령부》의 해체에 의한 인민적협상의료라고 믿는다. 따라서 우리로서는 에이 ...1—엽 708—수정1

《결의안》을 지지할수 없다. 그것은 이 《결의안》이 외국군대의 철거를 요구하고있지 않으며 그러므로 진정한 전의로는 배치되며 ...

위대한 수령 김일성동지께서

자이르공화국 대통령에게 축전을 보내시였다

킨샤사

자이르공화국 대통령

모부투 쎄쎄 세꼬 꾸꾸 느그벤두 와 자 방가 각하

나는 자이르공화국 국경절에 즈음하여 조선민주주의인민공화국 정부와 조선인민 그리고 나자신의 이름으로 당신과 귀국 전국접협의사회와 인민에게 열렬한 축하를 보냅니다.

근면한 자이르인민은 각하의 령도밑에 민족적독립을 공고히 하며 나라의 번영을 위한 사업에서 커다란 전진을 이룩하고있습니다.

조선인민은 자이르인민이 새생활창조에서 이룩하고있는 성과를 진심으로 기뻐하고있습니다.

나는 이 기회에 우리 두 나라 사이의 친선협조관계가 앞으로 더욱 강화발전되리라고 믿으면서 나라의 자주적발전을 위한 각하와 귀국인민의 투쟁에서 보다 큰 성과가 있을것을 축원합니다.

조선민주주의인민공화국 주석

김 일 성

1975년 11월 22일   평양

《유엔군사령부》를 해체하며 유엔의 기발밑에 남조선에 있는 모든 외국군대를 철거시켜야 한다

말리대표의 연설

【유엔본부 10월 30일 조선중앙통신 특파원발】28일 유엔총회 제30차회의 제1위원회에서 말리대표 마마가 팡께 연설하였다.

그의 연설은 다음과 같다.

유엔은 조선문제라는 복잡한 문제에 말려들게 되였으며 해방후 30년동안 조선은 그 인민들이 자주 표명한 의사와는 반대로 분렬로 남아있다. 이것 때문에 우리 기구는 자기의 의성과 권위를 손상하였다.

오늘 남조선에 있는 이른바 《유엔군》이 다름아닌 미국 《원정군》이라는것은 모든 사람들에게 명백하며 《유엔군사령부》가 이 《원정군》의 우두머리로 되여있

다는것도 명백하다. 우리로서는 우리 기구가 《유엔군》의 효과적 으로 통제하지 못하고있다는 사실을 감추려하지 않는다.

유엔은 정치협정을 공고한 관 화협정으로 전환시키며 조선의 자주적평화통일을 촉진시키는데 우리한 조건을 조성함으로써 조선문제를 해결할 수 있는 기회를 놓치지 말아야 한다.

바로 이를 위한 조치로 우리 나 라를 포함하여 40개 비동맹국 ...결의한 에이. 1—엽. 7 09에 모았당하였다.

1972년 7월 4일 조선의 북과 남은 나라의 자주적평화통일을 실현하려는 념원을 담은 남북공동성명을 발표하였다.

1973년 6월 23일에 조선민주주의인민공화국 주석이신 김일성원수님께서는 갈라진 조국통일방침을 다시금 천명하시였다.

다는것도 명백하다. 우리로부는 우리 기구가 《유엔군》을 효과적 으로 통제하지 못하고있다는 사 실을 감추려하지 않는다.

유엔은 정치협정을 공고한 평화협정으로 전환시키며 조선의 자주적평화통일을 촉진시키는데 유리한 조건을 조성함으로써 조선문제를 해결할 수 있는 기회를 놓쳐서는 안된다. 첫째로, 조선의 북과 남은 1972년 7월 4일 남북공동성명의 원칙을 엄격히 준수하면서 나라의 평화적통일을 위하여 노력하여야 한다.

우리 기구는 태양적 결정을 채택하고 조선의 자주적통일을 실현할수 있도록 도와주어야 할것이다. 이는 우리에게 우리가 《유엔군 (유엔군사령부》를 해체할것을 결정함으로써 시작하여 과정의 완성을 촉진할수 있다.

조선인민의 의사와 배치되는 조선의 분렬은 정당화될수 없다.

모잠비끄해방전선 위원장

사모라 모이세스 마셸동지 앞

나는 모잠비끄해방전선의 무장투쟁개시 10돐에 즈음하여 조선로동당 중앙위원회와 전체 당원들과 나자신의 이름으로 당신과 당신을 통하여 모잠비끄해방전선 중앙위원회와 귀 전선 전체 투사들에게 열렬한 축하를 보냅니다.

10년전 모잠비끄해방전선의 령도밑에 식민주의자들을 반대하는 무장투쟁개시는 모잠비끄인민의 반제민족해방투쟁에서 새로운 단계를 열어놓은 획기적인 사변이였습니다.

모잠비끄해방전선은 지난 10년간 자기 땅에서 뽀르뚜갈식민주의자들을 몰아내고 민족적독립과 해방을 이룩하기 위한 성스러운 투쟁에서 모잠비끄인민을 옳게 조직령도하여 빛나는 승리를 이룩하였습니다.

모잠비끄인민은 자기의 굴할줄 모르는 투쟁으로써 원쑤들을 막다른 궁지에 몰아넣었고 최근에는 모잠비끄의 완전독립에 관한 협정을 체결하였습니다.

이것은 모잠비끄해방전선의 주위에 굳게 단결하여 장기간의 피어린 무장투쟁을 벌려온 모잠비끄인민의 큰 승리이며 미제를 우두머리로 하는 제국주의자들과 식민주의자들에 대한 또하나의 커다란 타격으로 됩니다.

조선인민은 모잠비끄해방전선의 올바른 령도밑에 모잠비끄인민이 성스러운 반제민족해방투쟁에서 이룩하고있는 빛나는 승리를 자신의 성과와 같이 진심으로 기뻐하며 열렬히 축하하는바입니다.

우리 당과 인민은 지난날과 마찬가지로 앞으로도 제국주의와 식민주의를 반대하고 나라의 독립을 이룩하기 위한 모잠비끄해방전선과 모잠비끄인민의 정의의 투쟁을 모든 힘을 다하여 적극 지지성원할것입니다.

나는 조선로동당과 모잠비끄해방전선 그리고 두 나라 인민들사이의 친선단결이 앞으로 더욱 강화발전되리라고 믿으면서 민족적해방과 자유를 위한 모잠비끄인민의 앞으로의 투쟁에서 보다 새로운 승리가 있기를 축원합니다.

조선로동당 중앙위원회 총비서

김 일 성

1974년 9월 25일   평양

조선의 통일은 그 어떤 외세의 간섭도 없이 평화적으로 이룩되여야 한다

르완다대표의 연설

【유엔본부 10월 29일 조선중앙통신 특파원발】27일 유엔총회 제30차회의 제1위원회에서 르완다대표 ...연설하였다.

그의 연설은 다음과 같다.

오늘 조선문제가 우리 위원회에서 토의되고있다. 우리 위원회가 조선문제를 토의하게 된것은 이것이 처음이 아니다. 그것은 또한 마지막으로 될수도 없다. 왜냐하면 조선의 평화적이고 자주적인 통일을 달성하기 위한 길은 요원하기 때문이다.

우리 대표단은 자주적이며 평화적인 조선의 통일을 지지한다. 우리 대표단은 조선의 ...30년동안이나 ...

...조선인민자체의 렬망과 ...방침에 따라 달성되여야 한다. 그러나 이성과는 달리 ...남아 있다. 그것은 남조선에 외국군대가 주둔하고있기 때문이다.

...조선통일을 ...달성하기 위하여 첫째로, ...남북공동성명의 원칙에 기초하여 ...평화적으로 해결하여야 한다. 둘째로 ...조선에서 외국군대가 철거되여야 ...

우리 대표단은 ...조선의 자주적 평화통일을 촉진시키는데 유리한 조건을 조성할 에이.—1—엽. 709의 발기 나라 중의 하나이다.

우리 대표단은 1972년 7월 4일 남북공동성명에 표명된 원칙을 ...우리 대표단은 에이. ...1—엽. 708—...

우리는 남조선에 주둔하고있는 모든 외국군대의 철수를 요구한다

적도기네대표의 연설

【유엔본부 10월 29일 조선중앙통신 특파원발】27일 유엔총회 제30차회의 제1위원회에서 적도기네대표 ...연설하였다.

그의 연설은 다음과 같다.

오늘 남조선에 주둔하고있는 모든 외국군대의 철수를 요구하는것은 완전히 정당하다. 우리 대표단은 모든 외국군대가 조선반도에서 철거되여야 한다고 믿는다.

조선인민은 조선민주주의인민공화국 정부의 령도밑에 ...

...1972년 7월 4일 남북공동성명의 원칙을 엄격히 준수하여야 한다. 우리 대표단은 에이.—1—엽. 709의 발기 나라중의 하나이다.

...에이. 1—엽. 708—수정1... 우리 대표단은 1972년... 708—...

미군의 남조선주둔과 조선의 내정에 대한 미국의 간섭은 조선통일의 가장 큰 장애이다

리비아대표의 연설

소말리아에서 베르 베라세멘트공장착공식
성 대 히 진 행

모가디쇼에서의 보도에 의하면 소말리아의 베르 베라세멘트공장착공식이 10월 16일 현지에서 성대히 진행되었다.

모임장소정면에는 위대한 수령 김일성동지의 초상화와 그리고 소말리아최고혁명리사회 위원장 모하메드 시아드 바레의 초상화가 정중히 모셔져 있었다.

그리고 그 앞에는 우리 나라와 소말리아 두 나라 기발이 나란히 드리워져있었다.

모임장소에는 혁명의 위대한 수령 김일성동지의 현명한 령도밑에 우리 인민이 혁명과 건설에서 달성한 성과들을 보여주는 사진들이 전시되여있었다.

모임에서는 위대한 수령 김일성동지께 드리는 편지가 참가자들의 열광적인 박수속에 만장일치로 채택되었다.

모임은 소말리아최고혁명리사회 위원인 모하메드 알리 쉬레를 비롯한 관계부문일군들과 건설자들, 시민들과 학생들이 많이 참가하였다.

또한 여기에는 이 나라 주재 우리 나라 대사와 기술자들이 참가하였다.

모임은 우리 나라 애국가와 소말리아국가의 주악으로 시작되었다.

세멘트공장 지배인의 개회사에 이어 우리 나라 대사가 연설하였다.

다음으로 최고혁명리사회 위원인 모하메드 알리 쉬레가 연설하였다.

그는 자기의 연설에서 조선인민은 소말리아인민에게 이 공장을 비롯하여 종합전문학교, 관개시설물을 건설하여주는 등 많은 원조를 주고있으며 많은 트락토르를 보내주었다고 하면서 다음과 같이 계속하였다.

소말리아 최고혁명리사회와 인민은 우리의 념원과 목적을 지지하여주시며 우리에게 사심없는 원조를 주고계시는 경애하는 수령 김일성동지께와 위대한 수령님께서 령도하시는 조선인민에게 가장 충심으로 되는 감사를 드립니다.

그러면서 그는 조국통일을 위한 조선인민의 투쟁에 굳은 지지를 표시하였다.

그는 끝으로 《조선인민의 위대한 수령 김일성동지 만세!》, 《최고혁명리사회 위원장 모하메드 시아드 바레 소장 만세!》, 《소말리아인민과 조선인민사이의 위대한 친선 만세!》를 소리높이 불렀다.

【조선중앙통신】

조선문제를 토의하는 유엔총회

40여개국 공동결의안은 조선문제의 현실적이고 합리적이며 정당한 해결책을 제시하고있다
탄자니아대표의 연설

【유엔본부 10월 30일발 조선중앙통신 특파기자】 27일 유엔총회 제30차회의 제1위원회에서 탄자니아 대표는 조선문제에 관하여 다음과 같이 말하였다.

이로써 38도선은 그의이 없이 더욱이 단말하여서는 남아있을 수 없게 되었습니다. 조선 두 부분의 인위적분렬과 대립상태는 종식되고, 조선의 통일을 실현하여야 합니다.

유엔은 나라의 통일을 위한 조선 인민의 투쟁에 도움을 주어야 한다
세네갈대표의 연설

【유엔본부 10월 30일 조선중앙통신 특파원발】 10월 28일 유엔총회 제30차회의 제1위원회에서 세네갈대표 막탄 샤가 조선문제에 관하여 연설하였다.

남조선으로부터 외국군대를 철거시킬데 대한 조선인민의 립장을 전적으로 지지한다
우간다대통령이 강조

조선은 하나이며 절대로 둘로 갈라질수 없다
적도기네공화국 대통령이 강조

조선은 하나이다. 조선은 절대로 둘로 갈라질수 없다. 우리는 분렬을 반대한다.

【조선중앙통신】

또고정부가 남조선괴뢰도당과 외교관계를 단절
또고대통령이 인민련합 중앙위원회 비상회의를 소집

【평양 9월 19일발 조선중앙통신】 또고에서의 보도에 의하면 17일 오전 또고대통령 그나싱베 에야데마의 사회에 또고인민련합 중앙위원회 비상회의가 진행되었다.

비상회의는 또고대통령의 조선, 중국 방문결과에 대하여 토의하고 또고가 남조선괴뢰도당과의 외교관계를 단절하고 남조선괴뢰 《대사관》을 축출하기로 결정하였다.

또고정부가 남조선괴뢰도당과 외교관계를 단절하고 피회 《대사관》을 비워야 한다고 결정한 것은 조선을 또고공화국 대통령이 우리 인민의 정의로운 혁명위업을 지지하기 위한 적극적인 조치로 된다.

또고정부의 이 정당한 조치는 미제침략군의 남조선영구강점을 획책하면서 조선의 자주적평화통일을 극력 방해하고있는 미제국주의자들과 일본반동들의 책동에 2중의 박정피뢰도당에 대한 심대한 타격으로 된다.

또한 또고정부의 이 응당한 조치는 조선인민들에 대한 파쇼피뢰들을 장악하고 있는 한편 무슨서나 공화국정부를 흉포하고 있는 박정희살인악당이 오늘 세계인민들로부터 미움과 고립에처하고있다는것을 보여준다.

비반 사실로 날이 갈수록 공화국정부가 제3세계 인민들로부터 지지를 받고 있으며 조선인민의 정의로운혁명위업을 지지하는 경향은 높으며 세계인민들은 날로 바야 더 높아지며가고있다는것을 알려주고있다.

자이르인민은 조선의 통일은 조선인민 자신의 문제로서그 어떤 외세의간섭도 없이 자주적으로 해결되여야 한다고 인정한다
연회에서 한 모끌로 와 엠뽐보각하의 연설

조선민주주의인민공화국 정무원 부총리 외교부장 허담동지를 환영하여 베푼 연회에서

조선의 통일은 조선인민자신의 문제로서 그 어떤 외세의 간섭도 없이 자주적으로 해결되여야 한다고 인정하고있습니다.

앙골라 네또전대통령 동상   또고 에야데마전대통령 동상   꽁고 누구아비전대통령 동상

모잠비크 마쎌전대통령 동상   가봉 봉고전대통령 동상   에짚트 무바라크대통령 동상

225

인민예술가
건축도안창작가 김 영 섭

People's Artist
Architectural Drafter
Kim Yŏng-sŏp

공훈예술가
조각창작가 우 응 호

Meritorious Artist
Sculptor
U Ŭng-ho

공훈예술가
건축도안창작가 정 경 팔

Meritorious Artist
Architectural Drafter
Jŏng Kyŏng-pal

김일성상계관인, 인민예술가
조각창작가 류 하 룡

Kim Il Sung Laurel Wreath Winner
People's Artist
Sculptor
Ryu Ha-yŏl

인민예술가
조각창작가 김 성 시

People's Artist
Sculptor
Kim Sŭng-si

인민예술가
랍상창작가 백 만 길

People's Artist
Statue Artist
Paek Man-gil

김일성상계관인, 로력영웅, 인민예술가
조각창작가 오 대 형

Kim Il Sung Laurel Wreath Winner
Hero of Labor
People's Artist
Sculptor
O Dae-hyŏng

인민예술가
조각창작가 리 병 일

People's Artist
Sculptor
Ri Pyŏng-il

김일성상계관인, 로력영웅, 인민예술가
조각창작가 로 익 화

Kim Il Sung Laurel Wreath Winner
Hero of Labor
People's Artist
Sculptor
Ro Ik-hwa

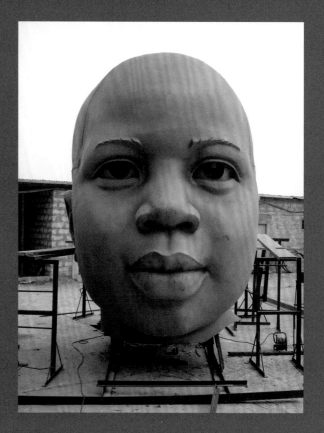

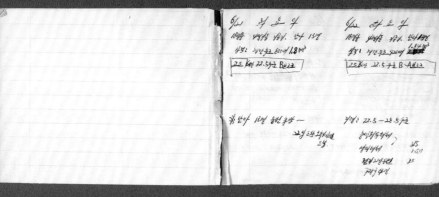

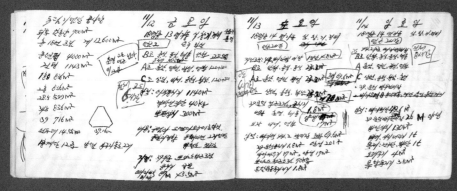

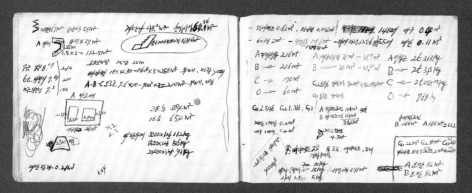

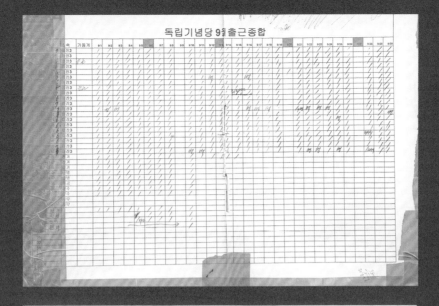

독립기념당 9월출근종합

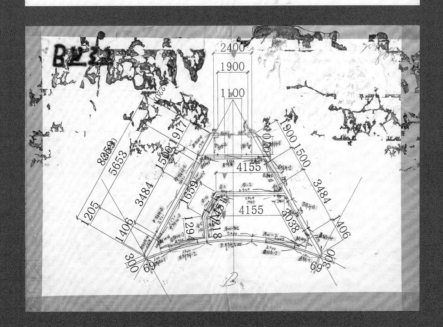

2010년 7월 근무부

A monument typifying Zimbabwe's freedom fighters graces the on-going construction work at Heroes' Acre—the national shrine which commemorates Zimbabwe's fallen heroes

Che Onejoon's
Archive of Korea in Africa

Joanna Lehan

Che Onejoon's skepticism of photography has paradoxically lived alongside his drive to master it. At 18 he attended the Korean Polytechnic School for its yearlong photography training, which left him wanting more academic rigor, yet grateful for the technical skills it gave him. These technical skills came in handy when he signed up for the Korean National Police for his compulsory military service. "It sounded easier than the army," Che jokes about his teenage naivete.

But once on this path, passion for the medium's possibilities took root. At 19, disguised as a journalist with a Nikon F4 around his neck, Che carried out his police duties at Seoul's largest political protests of the early 2000s. He says his job was to document unlawful activity, like the possession of weapons. He has heard that one of his photos may have caused the arrest of a friend of a friend, a student protest leader, but it's not possible to know if this is true. Still, he began to internalize the power of photography. He also began to understand its limits. Can a photo tell a complete, complex truth?

These questions deepened as later he is exposed to the writings of French philosopher Michel Foucault, whose provocative reframing of institutions and society inflected the documentary projects Che began on his own time. (Fig. 1) Initially taking advantage of his access to non-public sites as a member of the police force, Che turned his lens on interrogation and training rooms, courts and prosecutors' offices, presenting us with dispassionate images of the stages on which power performs. Other series focused on depopulated built environments that carry the legacy of the era of dictatorship—bunkers, unseen areas of the subway system. (Fig. 2) These images excavate layers of history, presenting them in all their stark facts, at least those that are visible.

Che's *Mansudae Master Class* (2013–ongoing), though made in a wholly different geographic setting, is an extension of this impulse to capture "hidden" architecture as evidence of political activities and societal structures on the Korean Peninsula. As websites pertaining to the DPRK are mostly blocked by the South Korean government, his research on the activities of Mansudae Art Studio required an international effort. Fueled at first by a grant from the Musée du quai Branly in Paris, he found that he also needed to employ the help of French and American researchers to vault the firewall of the 38th parallel. In February of 2013 he made his first trip to Africa, to Senegal, Democratic Republic of the Congo, Namibia, Botswana, and Zimbabwe, with a cinematographer, an assistant, and his large-format camera. That summer, funded by a grant from the Arts Council Korea, he returned to Namibia, Zimbabwe, and Senegal. Returning in 2015 he traveled back to Namibia and to Gabon. He's traveled to Africa four separate times so far, and visited nine countries.

The archive of images Che has assembled is impossible to summarize in brief. In each city he visited, the structures that he has depicted represent points of history in very different countries. The inception, and the reception, of these buildings and monuments also varies significantly. Perhaps it's best to simply begin at the beginning, then.

The monument that first spurred Che's interest is Africa's tallest, Senegal's African Renaissance Monument, completed in 2010. It was a project of president Abdoulaye Wade, constructed in bronze by Mansudae Overseas Projects at a $27-million-dollar cost. The monument features a family, rendered in the highly idealized style that is the hallmark of socialist realism: the angular muscularity of the shirtless man, center, with his right arm around the waist of a barely-enrobed, shapely woman. A baby perches on his powerful left bicep, pointing up and away to the future. The anachronistic style and bombastic scale of this monument is most certainly compelling.

In Che's photograph the Monument is decontextualized from the surrounding landscape and architecture. The steep hill on which the statue stands, commanding the skyline, is nearly leveled from the position Che makes his photograph. To return some context and extend his documentation of this site, Che included in his project the snapshots that local souvenir photographers have made of visiting tourists from a host of African countries. These images suggest the Monument's successful incorporation and acceptance as a site of African pride, yet don't tell the full story of the controversy and protests from various factions, well covered by the international press, that met the monument's construction.

This decontextualized depiction characterizes many of Che's photographs. A notable exception is the nearly romantic photograph of the Iavoloha Palace in Madagascar. One of the earliest projects, built in 1970 by North Korea as a gift to the so-called "Red Admiral" and Kim Il Sung admirer, president Didier Ratsiraka. In Che's photo the sprawling white palace nestled against a misty green hillside is foregrounded by farmlands and a rundown farmhouse. But those farmlands too, were in essence a gift from North Korea, who also built agricultural waterways in Madagascar.

Some of Che's photographs show the transformation of a site over time. Mansudae Art Studio had not yet completed the Namibian Independence Memorial Museum in the capital of Windhoek when Che first photographed it in 2013. In Che's photograph of the exterior of the Museum, a five-story golden-yellow triangular structure, which encompasses a cylinder, its stark modern lines a purposeful counterpoint to nearby German colonial structures in Windhoek, not included in Che's frame. An empty pedestal stands in front where once stood a German equestrian statue from 1912. When Che returned in 2015, the Museum was open, Mansudae Art Studio's bronze statue of Sam Nujoma sat on the once empty pedestal, and Che ventured inside. The exhibits in the museum: paintings, statues—some also produced by Mansudae Art Studio—tell unflinchingly of Namibia's brutal colonial past, and celebrate the heroes of independence. These interiors are reminiscent of the depopulated interior spaces in Che's photos in South Korea, stages for the telling of history.

The photographic archive also includes "The Gifts from Africa," objects that Che scanned in the North Korea Information Center of the National Library of Korea. Among them are many pages of a catalogue from the International Friendship Exhibition, a museum built by Kim Jong Il to display gifts the regime has received from foreign visiting dignitaries, a typical formality. The museum intends to evidence to its North Korean visitors Kim's global goodwill and respect.

Each page reproduced by Che is a still-life photo of a memento brought from Africa, some meaningful cultural keepsakes, others kitschy curiosities: a stuffed puffer fish from Equatorial Guinea, from the Nigerian Military Delegate an ornate white table clock shaped like a castle, which unfortunately resembles a wedding cake made in Disney World. Each gift in this catalog was photographed against surprisingly colorful, poppy backgrounds, amplifying the overall oddity of this document. Photographing this catalog was prohibited by the National Library so Che smuggled in a portable scanner, enjoying he says, this act of "stealing." The necessary low quality of the appropriated images underscores their status as restricted.

It's interesting to note that Che's photographic processes are heterogeneous and have fluctuated over the course of the project, though his organizing principal, charting the relationships between North Korean and African countries, has not. He has produced a film, which has been edited to both three-channel and single-channel formats, to suit both broadcast and museum presentations. He's made large-format photographs in black and white, and in color. He has also included additional appropriated materials: the photographs of itinerant African photographers at monument sites, and the records of North Korean workers in Africa found in the rubbish, and scans from North Korean newspapers.

Che has cited the Dusseldorf school photographers, led by Berndt and Hilla Becher, as an aesthetic influence, and this is legible in his serial, objective rendering of built structures, which point to political systems. The late Nigerian curator Okwui Enwezor in the essay for his exhibition *Archive Fever*, singled out Thomas Ruff from that group of photographers, which includes Thomas Struth and Candida Höfer. It is perhaps with Ruff's interest that Che is more closely aligned than with any of that cohort. Ruff, in such series as "Machines," made from images from an industrial catalog, and "Nudes" in which he appropriates and manipulates internet pornography, concerns himself with photographic archives, and in the limits and values of the photograph itself. As Enwezor puts it, "Ruff intervenes in the archive, making clear its status as an object of ethnographic and anthropological interest, as well as endowing it with epistemological and aesthetic functions."[1] So too, is the case with Che's "Gifts from North Korea," in which Che does not distinguish value between the images he made and the ones he unearthed. Each image shows an equally important facet of the cultural exchange he's pointing to, but no image is meant to stand alone. Instead, they accrue meaning in relation to the others; it is the archive he presents for us to consider.

Built architecture is a physical fact, and also an easily-read pictorial metaphor. The African metropolis, its monuments and architecture have been recorded by scores of contemporary African photographers, and the approaches and inherent metaphors in those bodies of work make interesting points of contrast to Che's project.

In Nigerian Andrew Esiebo's photographs of Lagos, architecture is a system, a kind of foil to human endeavor, but one over which Lagosians ingeniously triumph. In his 2015 photo of Tafawa Balewa Square, the monuments at the gates at the former site of the colonial Race Course, are cropped and blocked from full view by the rich visuality of a busy Lagos Boulevard, lively with vendors and pedestrians. In other images of highway overpasses, the subject is the people, walking through the clogged traffic, unstoppable.

In Guy Tillim's *Avenue Patrice Lumumba* (2009) the modernist built environments of post-colonial African countries are colored by the pathos of failed utopian ideas. This pathos is conveyed through crumbling infrastructure and somber colors.

David Goldblatt photographed architecture, as opposed to protests, to document the abomination of apartheid in South Africa. His book *South Africa: The Structure of Things Then* (1998) included photographs of churches, shops, monuments, all captured in what Goldblatt described as a "neutral optical effect." The images often carried detailed descriptive captions that serve to educate an international audience about the function of the structure. Goldblatt's long captions invited viewers to imagine how people lived under a regime whose racist machinations were laid out in byzantine rules, which shifted continually as apartheid was dismantled.

Che neither centers human activity, like Esiebo, nor assigns a poetic aesthetic to the sociopolitical as Tillim does, but like Goldblatt employs this neutral affect. The photos themselves don't tell or suggest the story of the history of each structure or state, they simply present them, full frame, depopulated and decontextualized from the surrounding city, accompanied by the simple facts of their year of construction, and when they were photographed. Whereas Goldblatt's photographs may have appeared neutral, their political statement was bold. Che, alternatively, despite what is in the photographs, is not illuminating the complex political histories of, for example, Botswana or Ethiopia. He is pointing instead to obfuscation itself, and the images, lacking in context, extend this theme.

"Gifts from North Korea" is in fact shorthand; through the 1980s North Korea did gift these monuments to countries, in a gesture of political allegiance to Non-Aligned African nations. However, as North Korea's economic position weakened, the monuments were actually paid for and commissioned from North Korea, who had proven, through their actual gifts, that it was an exceedingly skilled purveyor of ambitious yet economical architectural projects. (As one Al Jazeera podcaster put it, with excessive glibness: "Authoritarian statues are to North Korea what modular furniture is to Sweden,"[2]) Some of these structures, therefore, are political gifts, and some are in essence evidence of a side-door participation in the global economy.

But lingering on this point is not where Che has spent the bulk of his efforts, which have been—I underscore again—considerable. Crisscrossing the continent, Che's documentation of the African projects of North Korea's Mansudae Art Studio has been an arduous exercise in archive building.

Archives seem impersonal, emotionless, but of course we know they are not. They bear the same paradoxes of documentary photography, the appearance of irrefutable fact, which nonetheless is authored by an institution, or in this case an individual, with a singular situation in regard to history, to power.

The archives Che laboriously collects from those held by North Korea, and those embodied in Africa, chart the far reaches of a cold war. But the breadth of this collection of images and documents can also be seen

1.
Okwui Enwezor, *Archive Fever: The Use of the Document in Contemporary Art* (Göttingen: Steidl / ICP, 2008), 41.

2.
Kevin Herten interview with John Dell'Osso, "African Statues and North Korean Sanctions," May 21, 2021. *The Take*, Al Jazeera. Podcast Audio https://art19.com/shows/the-take?page=2.

as an effort of understanding, of reconciliation of facts. Like all archives they require that we consider the system that governs it, in this case the drive and intention of Che himself. And what could drive him to go to these lengths, to uncover for us things that are not commonly seen, and never thoroughly assembled together, except an abiding trust in the fact that truths should be in the light, should be recorded.

Che has traveled many thousands of miles over the course of years to assemble these documents. What they evidence is the reality of activities initiated only miles from his home in Seoul, which he otherwise would not be allowed to know. More than a cold war, they document a civil war. It is this chasm that Che strives so arduously to fill. If the photos alone, then, are neutral, and in what they show, so often so lacking in complex facts as to carry meaning insufficient to full understanding, then what has Che achieved? It is the archive itself, steeped in a sort of inchoate longing, and this fever of gathering, of a drive to piece it together, in the end, perhaps inconclusively—where the project's affect is most powerful.

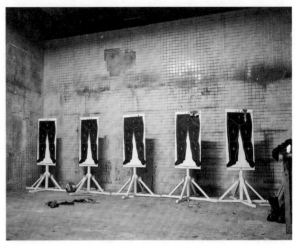

Fig. 1
Unallocated Space, Shooting Room#1, 2003, Digital C-print, 60×75cm

Fig. 2
Underground, Dongdaemun Station, 2005, Digital C-print, 155×195cm

The Gifts from Africa

Long-Distance Friendships. Rendering Visible the Invisible Stories in Che Onejoon's Practice

Inga Lāce

Introduction

My first encounter with Che Onejoon's work took place in a studio visit in Amsterdam several years ago. I remember watching fragments of his three-channel video *Mansudae Master Class* (2013–ongoing) and being for the first time introduced to the relationship between North Korea and African countries in the 1970s and 1980s. This relationship, which was slowly taking shape in front of me through Che's work, was two-fold. There were immense statues of African leaders made by North Korean artists and supported by the North Korean dictator, installed in many African countries, leaving a permanent marker in the public space and in the perception of its inhabitants. On the other hand, there was an impressive number of gifts, often small in scale, flowing back to Korea from, among others, the African leaders, meant for the dictator of North Korea. In Che's work the first part of this relationship is unveiled in a three-channel investigative documentary which we watched while engaging in a lively discussion about other instances of cultural diplomacy, the military relationship that often comes with it, as well as the politics of gift giving. Meanwhile, the second part of the relationship is manifested as photographic prints of exceedingly impractical objects symbolically containing an essence of the represented countries, in the series *International Friendship: The Gifts from Africa* (2017–2018).

While examining closely the *Mansudae Master Class* and *International Friendship: The Gifts from Africa* in this text, I will further delve into some parallel examples of cultural diplomacy between the Soviet Union and India, the traces of which I found in the archives in Latvia. This relationship broadens the context of Che's work and helps us to understand it in a context of lesser known or alternative political alliances bypassing the West, during the Cold War. Afterwards, I would like to turn to *My Utopia* (2018), a video installation by Che that follows the story of Monica Macias, the daughter of the then-Equatorial Guinean dictator, who grew up in North Korea. (Figs. 1 & 2) I will unveil how through Che's practice we can see the partially invisible processes rendered visible, like the policy of North Korea towards African countries, which was part of its competition with South Korea, the cultural exchange covering wider political, economic and military ties.

I call those relationships of cultural diplomacy and solidarity "long-distance friendships" as they occurred over distant geographies and express a certain mutuality. The notion of friendship is also a nod to the wide usage of this term in Soviet ideology. Through those relations, artworks, their styles, and materials were often physically transmitted and intellectually translated through long distances and different cultures and ideologies. The North Korea-made sculptures in Africa exhibit a socialist realist style that is characteristic to North Korea. The works by Indian artists in Latvia evoked manifold reactions, among them excitement and exoticizing. When objects of art and culture traverse long distances, what gets lost in translation and what new perceptions are evoked in the local audiences? Finally, opening the geopolitical perspective, I would like to stress that the "long-distance friendships" as they occur between countries, regions or individuals uncovered here propose alternative and lesser-researched geopolitical constellations that avoid the Western-centric point of view.

Mansudae Master Class

The three-channel documentary video *Mansudae Master Class* is one part of Che's long-term research and engagement with topics like cultural diplomacy, political and military alliances, state-controlled art and gift giving in politics, taking the history of North Korea as his starting point. The project owes its name to North Korea's creative agency Mansudae Art Studio, established in 1959 by order of Kim Il Sung, the founder and Supreme Leader of North Korea from 1948 till his passing away in 1994. Mansudae Art Studio is still one of the largest centres of art production in the world, with 700 artists and a staff of 4,000 working to produce paintings, posters and sculptures. It is government-run and used primarily to promote the state's leaders and military, but the studio also accepts commissions from international clients.[1] The studio has also since the 1970s been engaged in building monuments and statues in African countries, which served as "gifts" from North Korea. As the former North Korean director of Central Africa affairs reveals in Che's documentary, "a sub-bureau under the Mansudae Art Studio functions there almost as a separate organization. When it first started overseas projects in 1974, it only received travel expenses. The monuments in Ethiopia were built free of charge because president Mengistu Haile Mariam was a pro-North Korean leader. However, in the mid-1980s this activity became the main source of earning foreign currency, as recipient countries began to be billed."

In Che's documentary we see the juxtaposition of fragments from African liberation moments in Africa, North Korean propaganda films and recent interviews made by Che with local artists, curators, and political activists in different African countries. The editing of the three synchronized channels moves dynamically between different times and places, between artworks, historic and recent documentary footage, giving an impression of the multiplicity of possible perspectives on the same situation, depending on where one stands ideologically, and what power, information and access they have. For example, at the beginning of the film a grey cloth is taken off the statue of Joshua Nkomo, Zimbabwean vice-president from 1990 until his death in 1999. The scene takes place in the Natural History Museum of Zimbabwe and is shown from three different angles and distances, revealing, on the first screen, two blue-coated workers engaged in the process of uncovering the sculpture; on the second, a close-up of the sculpture; and, on the third, just the head of the sculpture. A moment later, the same sculpted head of Nkomo appears in the middle of two images of popular protests, only to be then replaced by the man himself speaking amidst the images of the violent action on the screens to either side.

The subtle choreographic rhythm of the film intensifies when the camera follows the monuments in the public space, playing with close-ups and images disappearing from one screen only to reappear on another. The rhythmic liveliness of the editing is even further emphasized by the audio composition. The gifts in the shape of the grand monuments are, of course, far from invisible, but they do work as a cover to other arrangements that have existed between the many African countries and North Korea, including the training of African troops, arms deals, as well as economic ties.

Commenting on the monumental nature of the exchange, the *Mansudae Master Class* three-channel video is often shown on TV screens elevated on gray pedestals with a slope towards the backside, reminding viewers of the simple shape of the base of a monument. Che's exquisite scenography mirrors the subject matter of the work. The content of the work is just as important as the symbolic spatial gestures surrounding it which will affect the movement of the bodies in space and the perception of the content. The installation also contains photographs of the monuments and their vast surroundings, most of the time without any people. Contrary to the video, the images are eerie, because their embodied desertedness making one wonder whether the monuments have ever put their roots down into the daily lives of the people, whether the squares around them are ever populated with life, or whether are they only activated through moments of political exchange.

According to Che, there are two main reasons behind North Korea's support for African countries. First, North Korea wanted to spread its "Juche" ideology created by Kim Il Sung to the newly independent African countries, because it wanted Africa to have a similar ideology and political system. Second, North Korea needed to gain support from the African countries at the United Nations so that they could receive more votes against the stationing of the U.S. Army and the United Nations Command in South Korea. Both the U.S. Army and the United Nations Command in South Korea have been the biggest threats to North Korea since the end of the Korean War in 1953.[2]

Furthermore, as the UN experts state, eleven African countries—Angola, Benin, Botswana, Democratic Republic of Congo, Eritrea, Mali, Mozambique, Namibia, Tanzania, Uganda, and Zimbabwe—are suspected of having military ties to Pyongyang until recently.[3] Many of them are quietly resisting or ignoring the pressure of the US to cut ties, in the meantime giving North Korea the necessary time and means to continue to develop their nuclear missile program.

1.
Sara Boboltz, "North Korea's Arts Scene Is Just As Mysterious As The Nation Itself," *Huffington Post*, Sep. 22, 2015, https://www.huffpost.com/entry/north-korea-art-scene_n_55ef4c0ee4b093be51bc9a0a.

2.
Jaewook Lee, "Onejoon Che's Objects of Counter-Hegemonic History: The International Friendship," *TK-21*, July 2, 2020, https://www.tk-21.com/Onejoon-Che-s-Objects-of-Counter?lang=fr.

3.
David Pilling, Adrienne Klasa, and Katrina Manson, "US steps up pressure on African countries to cut North Korea ties," *Financial Times*, January 29, 2018, https://www.ft.com/content/bda4e76e-0440-11e8-9650-9c0ad2d7c5b5.

A Parallel Friendship

That sort of search for political allies involving culture and art as mechanisms, reminds me of another "friendship" between countries—the Soviet Union's relationship with India during the Cold War. While working on an exhibition at the Art Museum RIGA BOURSE in Riga, Latvia, and looking through the archives of exhibitions held there during Soviet times, I came across many exhibitions that were devoted to art from India, Congo, and Central Asian Soviet Republics. Besides the list of exhibitions and folders containing related correspondence and media clippings with reviews in Latvian newspapers, there was rarely any photo documentation of either the works or the opening event. Moreover, the archivist admitted that museum staff organized exhibitions as a duty towards the all-powerful Soviet art system, while truly desiring to exhibit art from Western Europe.[4] The exhibition of Contemporary Paintings and Prints from India which took place in 1974, for example, showed 54 works from the 1940s and 1950s from the collection of the Moscow State Museum of Oriental Art, a gift from India to the Soviet Union. The works were categorized by a variety of themes, and styles of painting and printmaking.[5] Among them were works from artists like Jamini Roy, one of the most famous pupils of Abanindranath Tagore, founder of the influential Bengal School of Art, who alongside other artists advocated in favour of a modern, nationalist Indian art, or Kattingeri Krishna Hebbar, known for his India-themed artworks. In the 1987 exhibition, the works were brought over from Deli Contemporary National Gallery, as part of the larger Festival of India celebrations in the Soviet Union, of which art was just one component. A review reads "We did not know the names of those Indian artists [...] Strange were the symbols, the ancient Hindu signs that we saw depicted in paintings and sculptures. But close and understandable was the sparkling color—so vivid and bright. Also understandable is the spirituality so strongly emphasized in the 20th century Indian art and sought out by people all over the world."[6]

The Festival of India, which took place in the Soviet Union, mainly in Moscow, but, as described earlier, in Riga as well, a counterpart of a similar Festival of the Soviet Union held in India that same year. *The New York Times* described the festival in India in the following way: "The occasion is a huge Festival of the Soviet Union mounted this week by Prime Minister Rajiv Gandhi and Nikolai I. Ryzhkov, the Soviet Prime Minister. The celebration, an example of the politics of culture, has upstaged the recent talk about improved relations with the United States and thrown American officials on the defensive. Indeed many Western diplomats say that Moscow has again proved itself more adept than Washington at wooing India."[7]

The cultural events were part of a larger strategic, military, economic and diplomatic relationship between India and the USSR during the Cold War, beginning in the 1950s, notably the most successful of the Soviet Union's attempts to foster relationships with the Third World countries. Soviets acted as peace broker between India and Pakistan over the Kasmhir territorial dispute; they also gave India substantial economic and military assistance during the Khrushchev period; and were neutral during the Sino-Indian war of 1962, putting at risk their own relationship with China.

The Festival of India in 1987 and different exhibitions and events in the Soviet Union preceeding it took place at the height of the international Cold War and were a direct product of its politics. What was visible, in part, in the exhibitions of art from India, was a diversity of styles, inspired by Indian traditional art and Western painting, and searching for unique expressions by individual artists.

The production at Mansudae Art Studio has, however, continued even after the collapse of the Cold War order, until nowadays serving the North Korean government as a collective machinery of state art. The extreme isolation of North Korea and state control have directed the socialist realist output of Mansudae Art Studio only through state-accepted channels. And even though it has been shown internationally recently or gained attention through the work of contemporary artists like Che Onejoon, the work at the studio remains largely anonymous and more valued than artistic creativity are tradition, repetition and copying.

Gifting Back

The other part of the project, mentioned at the beginning of this essay, is *International Friendship: The Gifts from Africa*, which presents the gifts given to the North Korean

4.
Author's conversation with Vineta Beržinska, Head of Scientific Document Center at the Latvian National Museum of Art, July 4, 2018.

5.
M. Zaķe, "Indijas māksla Rīgā" [Art from India in Riga] in *Literatūra un Māksla* [*Literature and Art*], June 8, 1974.

6.
Magda Priedīte, "Indijas māksla Latvijā" [Indian Art in Latvia] in *Zvaigzne* [*Star*], February 20, 1988.

7.
Steven R. Weisman, "New Delhi Warms to Soviet Cultural Festival," *New York Times*, November 27, 1987, https://www.nytimes.com/1987/11/27/world/new-delhi-warms-to-soviet-cultural-festival.html.

dictators by the leaders of the rest of the world. In 1978, Kim Il Sung built the International Friendship Exhibition Hall, a large exhibition complex in Myohyangsan (Mt. Myohyang) in North Korea, currently serving as a public museum. The six-story building enclosing 28,000 square meters holds the main hall, which displays gifts sent to Kim Il Sung from national political parties, national leaders, and political figures, as well as an annex with gifts to Kim Jong Il, in total more than 270,000 items.[8] Looking at the donated objects, one can also notice a spider web rendering visible the ties the North Korean leadership has with the other oppressive powers.

In a library in South Korea, Che found a book that holds images of the gifts. The book was only available for reading, no copying or scanning was allowed. Heedless of the library's prohibition, Che used a portable hand scanner to scan the images in such a way that errors in movement meant some images have lost some of the symbolic importance that the museum and the gifts it houses are supposed to convey. Taking this work further, Che 3-D printed tangible objects from the low-quality scans. The process of copying and new reproduction brings to the fore the question of the uniqueness of the gift. From an object of symbolic and actual value it becomes a national souvenir which can be reproduced en masse.

I first saw the prints in Che Onejoon's studio. The only common characteristics between the objects are their obvious impracticality and their seeming importance, as they are supposed to contain the essence of the countries they represent. Wonder at the peculiarity of each of the objects while one looks at them in Che's rendering is soon substituted by pondering on the larger political processes they represent.

The collective production of state art at the Mansudae Art Studio, as well as official state gifts, are a field of art production usually not considered interesting for the contemporary art field. Instead of art museums, contemporary art exhibitions or biennales, they circulate in their own networks of state commissions, official representation events and embassies, serving less as art and more as a political tool. Through reproducing the objects, documenting the monuments, and delving into a discussion about them with different parties, Che brings their distribution and the logic and interests behind them to the contemporary art field, juxtaposing

historical, political, economic and visual analysis, which extends much further than any single field of studies would get.

Finding Your Own Utopia
This is where I would like to discuss another work by Che—a three-channel video in a documentary theatre format called *My Utopia*, inspired by the story of Monica Macias. (Fig. 3) She was the daughter of the first president of Equatorial Guinea and spent 16 years in exile in Pyongyang, due to a coup that took place in her own country in 1979. After the death of her father, North Korean leader Kim Il Sung raised her as his own daughter, since the two regimes were friendly. As the story in the film evolves, we see protagonists expressing their curiosity towards each other's skin colours and languages, foreign to each of them. A visible other in the rather homogenous North Korean society, Macias ultimately leaves the country for China, then Spain, the United States and South Korea. Having been educated under the heavy blanket of North Korean propaganda, as well as socialist and anti-Western ideologies, she is shocked to learn other possible points of view, including the South Korean perspective of the Korean War, which leaves her forever confused, displaced and searching for "her own utopia," as she explains in the film, beyond national belonging, race, or language, adding "people cannot be free from the memories of their upbringings." Monica is, however, trying to become free by moving and never settling in North Korea again.

Besides the difficulties of searching for one's own identity after experiencing extremely different contexts, the film *My Utopia* also highlights starkly the personal aspect in the political friendship between states and, ultimately, the dictators who run them, and we see that not only are they ready to support each other economically or politically, but also by bringing up one another's children.

Conclusion
I would like to go back to the beginning of this essay of discovering the mutual cultural, political, military and economic relationship between North Korea and African countries through Che's works. North Korea's public monuments in African countries or places like the Inter-

8.
Che Onejoon, *Mansudae Master Class*, 2013– ongoing, Three-channel HD video installation, 40min 50sec.

national Friendship Exhibition in Myohyangsan are part of the official visual culture and are right in front of us, yet are often left unanalysed. However, exactly through those objects the cultural diplomacy emerges as the smokescreen for heavily politically charged "friendships" characterized in this case by dictatorial alliances, based on military, political and economic support between countries. Che is only starting with the "soft" cultural layer of those relationships to quickly unveil the often-invisible ties that lay beyond. To dialogue with North Korean-African friendship, I brought in the Soviet Union-India relationship that reveals itself through museum archives in Latvia. Both of those relationships point towards the Cold War alliances that were bypassing the West. Supporting the African struggle for independence, or strengthening the Indian political position regionally, those efforts were at the same time coming from ultimately anti-democratic regimes.

Analysing those examples, an important question arises—could there be alternative friendships—different networks between countries that do not only cover invisible power structures? Is it possible to escape the gift-giving logic that presumes that the other one is already indebted? Is an ultimately equal exchange possible? Perhaps, as the work of Che does so thoroughly, we should start by understanding what lies beyond the transmission of cultural gifts, first, and use that knowledge to reformulate our future long-distance friendships.

Fig. 1
My Utopia, 2018, Single-channel HD video, 27min 35sec

Fig. 2
Installation view of *My Utopia*, 2018, Busan Biennale 2018, *Divided We Stand*, Museum of Contemporary Art Busan, Busan, South Korea

Fig. 3
My Utopia, 2018, Three-channel HD video installation, 21min 43sec

Ghosts and Idols,
or the Politics of Potentiality

Seon-Ryeong Cho

As a subject of art, North Korea has the paradox that it is impossible to confirm its existence but overflowing with meanings. The meanings generally oscillate between a nationalist dream cultivated under the name of the "lost half (of Korea)" and a leftist's yearning for the self-sufficient socialist model. Is there a way to represent North Korea without stumbling over the meshwork of these two desires? And can the representational method create a space of active interpretation that enables the expansion of experiences and perceptions of the nation? In recent years, Che Onejoon's work on the North Korea-Africa relationship, specifically *Mansudae Master Class* (2013–ongoing), offers a very interesting answer to this challenging question.

First, Che's work consistently maintains an objective stance without empathizing with North Korea. It exhibits no nationalist, socialist, or humanistic perspective that we are familiar with. Of course, this objective stance is not exclusive to Che's work. Many artists (mainly foreign photographers) try to eliminate the possibility of personal interpretation or empathy as much as possible to remove the images already overlaid on North Korea. They make a subjective choice to see North Korea as it is. However, their photographs and Che's work are different. Before we analyze this difference, let's bear in mind one simple fact. Because Che is a South Korean, it is impossible for him to see North Korea as it is, so the term subjective choice is virtually meaningless for him. Instead, Che decided to see North Korea through a third party, Africa.

The artist came up with the idea of *Mansudae Master Class* after by chance catching a news item about the African Renaissance Monument built by North Korea in Senegal. Since starting this project in February 2013, Che has visited thirteen cities in nine African countries including Zimbabwe, Senegal, Gabon, Democratic Republic of Congo, Botswana, Namibia, and Ethiopia.

He photographed the statues and monuments constructed by North Korean artists from Mansudae Art Studio. In addition, he collected other relevant materials, archival footage, photographs, and interviewed various people, including writers, curators, administrators, and politicians.

The artist presented the outcome as a three-channel video installation for exhibitions and a single channel video for broadcasting. In addition to this, a series of photos, sculptures, and archives are also included in the installation work. The artist photographed the monuments separately with a large format camera. Che recorded other buildings built by local architects to compare with the ones made by North Koreans. After Che returned to South Korea, the artist produced miniature replicas of the large African statues built by North Koreans.

Che's works deserve recognition for the efforts he made. His work is also valuable as it focuses on North Korea-Africa relations, which have been rarely discussed so far. But what perspective does this work offer on North Korea? What kind of space for interpretation does the form and content of Che's work give? It is relatively difficult to answer this question. Above all, the relationship that this work focuses on draws an entirely different trajectory from the worthy history we have believed. The so-called "Juche" style is often regarded as an undeveloped socialist realist style. This Juche style was applied to erecting statues and monuments in African countries (mainly dictatorships). We (those who are somewhat progressive audiences and critics from South Korea) feel far from moved or satisfied by the Juche aesthetic.

The statues and monuments are ridiculously large or exaggeratedly heroic or phallic. For example, the African Renaissance monument, erected by the North Korean artists in Dakar in 2010, is a 52-meter tall sculpture that costs 1-2 million US dollars a year to maintain. A muscular man gazes into space with a triumphant expression, holding a baby in one arm and embracing a woman in the other. The line from the woman's arm to the baby's arm is almost straight. It seems to create a healthy and progressive impression, but the shape itself is the embodiment of masculine heroism and nationalism.

Africans interviewed by Che were not happy with the monuments or statues made by North Korea. In Zimbabwe, North Korea trained the 5th Brigade (an infantry brigade of the Zimbabwe National Army) that led to the massacre of Ndebele civilians. They were angry that North Korea also made a statue of former vice-president Joshua Nkomo in the city of Bulawayo in the Matabeleland region, Nkomo's political base. The son of Nkomo said that the North Korean statue was insult more than anything, claiming, "government was able to offer that project to a local artist or other African countries."

What, then, does *Mansudae Master Class* present through those bizarre sculptures don't exactly please people, either aesthetically or politically? To interpret this work, I would like to find some clues in Che's previous works. Starting with *Texas Project* (2004–2008), *Undercooled* (2006–2008), *Unfinished Project_Island* (2005–2007), *Townhouse* (2006–2010), and *Spinning Wheel* (2011), the artist has constantly been interested in certain exceptional things. The sites that Che photographed were not well known to the general public. These locations are often concealed or accessible only to a few people. These include a red-light district for the U.S. military in South Korea (Fig. 1), the protective walls and anti-tank defensive line built in northern Gyeonggi Province, abandoned U.S. military camps in South Korea, underground bunkers, and an air raid shelter built during the military dictatorship period in South Korea. These things generally played a special role in the history of the Cold War and the division between North and South Korea. They are often revealed by accident. For example, in *Undercooled*, we see military facilities accidentally found during the construction of a new apartment complex. (Fig. 2) In *Unfinished Project_Island*, a bunker was found during the construction of the Yeouido Bus Transfer Center. (Fig. 3) In *Townhouse*, a U.S camp became accessible when the American soldiers stationed there were dispatched to the Iraq War. (Fig. 4)

When a concealed object emerges by accident, the original meaning that has been given to the object disappears. In other words, the disappearance of meaning takes place after an object no longer serves its original function. When that object's existence reveals itself, its purpose disappears. In this regard, the objects Che photographed are not romantic ruins that evoke melancholy. These are the paradoxical sceneries that emerge through the transformation of the objects' functions. For example, in a photo from the *Undercooled*

series, Che took a picture of an apartment construction site where an underground bunker was found half-exposed in a pile of dirt. With a cloudy sky in the background, the time of day is not clear because there is no light or shadow. (Fig. 5)

These two locations (the military bunker and the construction site) meet by chance like Comte de Lautréamont's famous "chance juxtaposition of a sewing machine and an umbrella on a dissecting table." When the bunker or barrier becomes useless, the meaning given to those objects and places (maybe excessively) in the history of division and the Cold War becomes ineffective. Che's photographs retrospectively ask the meaning of a specific object where the original function has ceased. However, the paradox of these objects is that their temporality is not linear. The objects were built for a future event but have never been used. The underground bunkers and barriers captured in *Undercooled* and *Unfinished Project_Island* were created in preparation for a potential war that could break out on the Korean Peninsula. However, there has been no hot war since the Korean Armistice Agreement was signed, and the objects lost their function, becoming useless.

The air raid shelter, anti-tank defensive line, and bunkers were never used as they were intended. These objects existed only for some possible future scenarios (such as war). The potential war is fictional because it has never occurred, but it is by no means a subjective fantasy. Time is strange because the meaning of the objects has a "future perfect" tense, meaning that they were built in preparation of the potential outbreak of war in the future. When the concealed objects reveal themselves in a useless way, the future suddenly becomes the past perfect tense. In other words, they show a past event that has already ended.

Mansudae Master Class can be seen as an extension of Che's previous photographic works, yet weaving a more multifaceted dynamic on North Korea. North Korea is an almost entirely closed place and absolutely forbidden territory to South Koreans due to the national division and the Cold War on the Korean peninsula. Except for a very few, no South Korean can enter North Korea. And no one can confirm the reality of it. In this respect, it is natural that Che turned his curiosity to North Korea. As Che said, Africa was primarily a way of bypassing the fact that he could not directly travel north of the DMZ.

However, *Mansudae Master Class* raises more issues than that. It is not just about being on the trail of North Korea in Africa. *Mansudae Master Class* explores the unexpected complexity of the relationship between these two places. It is a result of Che's effort to see the history of the Korean division more globally. It presents a new perspective on interpreting history through relations among North Korea, Africa, and South Korea. As mentioned above, the photographs and sculptures are included in the work. However, in this article, I will mainly focus on the video, because this plays a primary role in *Mansudae Master Class*. For Che, video was a relatively new medium in the 2010s. I am going to interpret the video in connection to his previous photographic works.

Mansudae Master Class shows interviews, original footage, and found footage related to North Korea on three screens. The images of the monuments and statues made by North Korean artists, Kim Il Sung's speech, the footage from (North) Korean Central Television, the photographs from present-day Africa, and the interviews all form an intricate pattern on the three screens. The screens sometimes go black at the same time. Che already tested this three-channel video format in *Spinning Wheel* (2011). In this work, the interviews with the residents of Mullae-dong, the scenery of that neighborhood and a fictional story played out by actors are shown separately on each screen. (Fig. 6) However, *Mansudae Master Class* has a relatively unified narrative across the screens. Like *Spinning Wheel*, it consists of three parts: the audio, the image, and the landscape. However, unlike *Spinning Wheel*, these parts intersect with one another as they cross the screens. Although Che made a single-channel video for broadcast, he aimed for a three-channel video format from the beginning of the production. When Che went to Africa, he also took three cameras.

Photography can freeze time and overlap different times even in a single image. This is because what is visible can paradoxically designate what is not visible. On the other hand, a video has the property of continually passing by, so it lacks the ability to freeze time unless it is specially edited that way. However, video is an appropriate medium for giving a certain depth to stories and speech. Also, video can intersect the existence and the absence in another way while showing the sequence of events.

The use of three-channel video turns the temporal into the spatial, cutting the flow of the video. Yet, such a cut is still presented within the flow of images. In the end, the three-channel video format is a useful method to produce various meanings in the intersection of objects, spaces, images, and language as it weaves the relationship between the two strains—the flow (depth, narrative, and syntagm) and the cut (surface, relation, and paradigm). These two strains of flow and cut do not correspond to the role assigned to the speech and image in traditional documentaries.

In traditional documentaries, speech functions to explain images. In the so-called "post-documentary," on the other hand, the two are considered equal and independent elements. However, Che's work rarely uses poetic and suggestive expressions. In this respect, it is difficult to view Che's film as a typical post-documentary. I would call *Mansudae Master Class* a "materialistic documentary" as it weaves relationships among objects, images, spaces, and languages.

The meeting between Africa and North Korea in *Mansudae Master Class* is just as accidental as the meetings shown in the previous photographic works. Of course, it can be said that the historical fact of the Non-Aligned Movement brought about the meeting of North Korea with Africa. However, it seems strange to us that the Mansudae Art Studio, which has made Juche style art, has also created heroic monuments or statues of African dictators. South Korean audiences become embarrassed when the style of Juche, close to kitsch, combines the physical appearance of Africans with the heroic monumental style invented by the West. Listening to the interviewees' comments does not resolve that feeling of embarrassment. The interviewers do not consistently evaluate the work made by the artists of Mansudae Art Studio. Some Africans are angry and criticize the statues for political reasons. Some believe the statues don't reflect who they really are. Conversely, some say that North Koreans are agile and genuine, and their work is the best.

Among the utterances from various interviews, some statements suggest important keywords for interpreting

Fig. 1
Texas Project, Hyangkinae, 2004, Digital C-print, 118×150cm

Fig. 2
Undercooled, Protect Line #4, Uijeongbu, 2007, Digital C-print, 120×180cm

Fig. 4
Townhouse, Camp Giant, Paju, 2009, Detailed image from the triptych, Digital C-print, 120×540cm

Fig. 3
Unfinished Project_Island, Transit Transfer Center 2006. 5 (Ground) Bunker #7 2005.05 (Underground), Digital C-print, 113×78cm

Fig. 5
Undercooled, Eunpyeong-gu Newtown #1, Gupabal, 2007, Digital C-print, 120×163cm

Fig. 6
Spinning Wheel (part1), Interview, 2011, HD video installation, 7min 28sec
Spinning Wheel (part2), Landscape, 2011, HD video installation, 7min 28sec
Spinning Wheel (part3), Spinning Wheel, 2011, HD video installation, 14min 50sec

Fig. 7
Feng Shui (Theory of divination based on topography), Grave of Dictator Park's Father: The Shape of a Golden Crow Pecking a Body, Gyongbuk Gumi, 2011, Digital C-print, 122×200cm

The Gifts from Africa

the work. They are the remarks of an Islamic imam and a Namibian journalist. The imam sits with tribal believers and criticizes the Senegalese government for entrusting North Korea with the construction of the African Renaissance Monument. One of the reasons for his criticism is religion. He says, "Statues are not allowed in Islam." This is the well-known Islamic law against idolatry.

In a sense, the entire *Mansudae Master Class* is about idols. This is because the statues and monuments themselves are idols, and North Korea itself is known as a country in which people worship Kim Jung Un's family as god-like idols. Che's interest in idols is not sudden. This could already be seen in *Spinning Wheel* and the *Feng-Shui* (Asian geomancy) series on the statue of Park Chung-hee and his father's grave, etc. (Fig. 7) At first glance, idols seem to be full of meaning, but they are actually empty. The powerful materiality of an idol, its exaggerated presence, is a means of concealing the fact that it really lacks an intrinsic meaning. After all, an idol has an exaggerated appearance but no significant connotations.

On the other hand, in his interview, a Namibian journalist John Grobler says the opposite: "I think it was a longing for Marxism that is brighter or better than it really is." This remark means a lot to South Korean progressive liberals—the primary audience of this work. Socialism was a dream and ideal that they could not achieve. Some South Koreans' yearning for socialism was like a ghost wandering through history for a long time. It was a specific ideology that went around without substance, like a rumor that the entire new city of Ilsan was a vast military facility built in preparation for a future resumption of the Korean War. Contrary to idols, a ghost has no substance but exaggerated connotations. A person who dies an untimely death of unnatural causes becomes a ghost and wanders around this world because he has a mission to complete. When the ghost deciphers its own meaning, the ghost disappears.

In short, we can interpret *Mansudae Master Class* as a story about "Idols and Ghosts." Although idols and ghosts have opposite natures, they are also different names for the same entity. What is a ghost in South Korea is an idol in Africa. The excess of meanings given to ghosts is paired with the excess of existence given to idols and each cancels the other out. In this respect, *Mansudae Master Class* is a work that reveals the reality of ghosts through idols. This perspective is also the key to deciphering the meaning of the 3-D miniature sculptures included in Che's installation. In Africa, what used to be a sign of great heroism turns into a hobby of collecting trophies when it comes to Korea, and a status shift that the artist has continuously pursued occurs.

The dream of socialism and its artistic style called "socialist realism" were realized in Africa in a way no one wanted (from the perspective of South Korean progressive liberals). The material reality (idol) of huge statues and monuments is paired with a fictional entity (ghost) called "Utopian North Korea or Socialist South Korea." This is how South and North meet in Che's video. Through Africa, regarded as a third party, two Koreas meet at the interface between the real and the fictional. In a sense, Africa is no longer a third party; South Korea is. The North Korea-Africa relationship is primary. In other words, Che's work is not just about North Korea and South Korea, but also a story about Africa. Rather than having one part as the center and placing the rest in orbit around it, a complex and dynamic relationship between the three (North Korea, Africa, and South Korea) is woven. Virtually any place can be the third party (North Korea-Africa, North Korea-South Korea, and Africa-South Korea) Any permutation of relationships is possible.

Che's old works show how time erases the meaning of particular objects. On the other hand, *Mansudae Master Class* shows a more complex method of deconstructing and reconstructing time and space while still an extension of the exploration of the same subject matter. Not only the dislocation of time, but the dislocation and junction of space occur in *Mansudae Master Class*. For the majority of South Koreans, Africa is a place with few pre-established meanings, because there is no special historical link with South Korea. In other words, Africa as the bracketed third party reveals coincidence and meaninglessness removing the "excessive meaning" saturated in the historical relationship between South Korea and North Korea. It is combined with the fact that the statues and monuments constructed by North Korea are kitsch, that is, surplus objects that are close to meaningless.

In the end, the objective stance shown by *Mansudae Master Class* is not the result of a personal will to see North Korea as it is. Humans are a species that cannot stop giving meanings and interpretations to objects, spaces, and images. The only point where their meanings or interpretations disappear is when they become useless. The idea of socialism, which has haunted South Korea, turns out to be "useless" in Africa where it is realized.

However, this bitter manifestation does not boil down to nostalgia or depression. The disappearance of meaning is not a melancholic event that blocks the future but can become raw material for a new history. *Mansudae Master Class* shows an event in which the excess of meaning is offset by the excess of existence, which becomes the starting point for weaving a new history. The work of emptying meaning, more precisely, the work of capturing the space and time from which meaning has been emptied, frees history from the trap of the aesthetics of loss and mourning while dissolving the obsession with unfulfilled dreams.

The "objective stance" in Che's work does not come from a lack of empathy or of perspective, but from a new perspective on Korea's division history. History is not a repetition of what is already known, but an event newly constructed at an unexpected point by accidental discovery. This perspective constitutes what can be called "the politics of potential" throughout Che's work. A new reality can be made through the shift of functions and meanings. The fiction of history revealed here is not the opposite of fact, but another name for possibility.

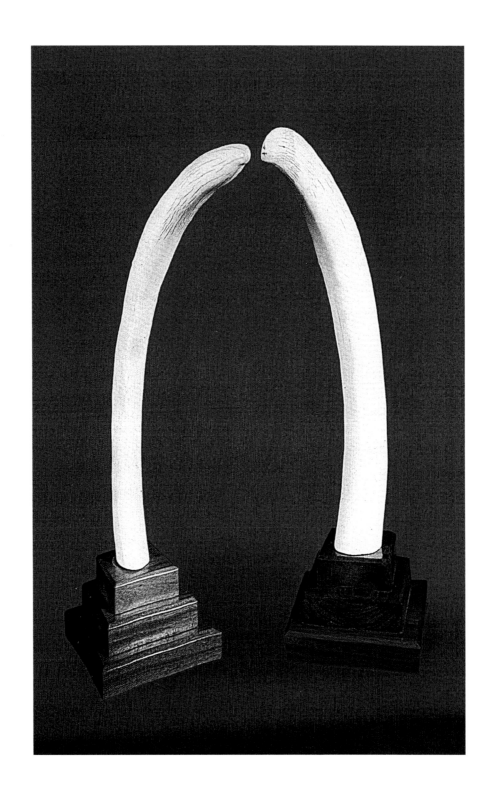

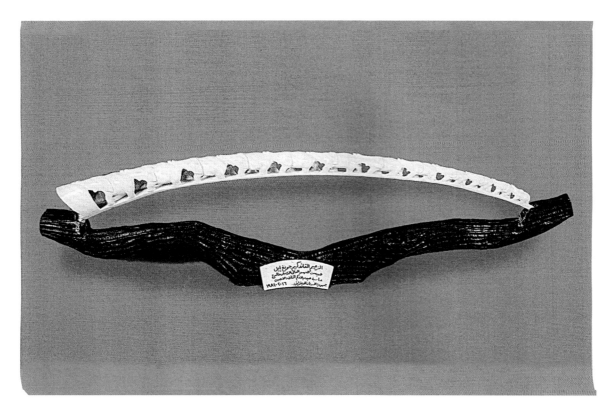

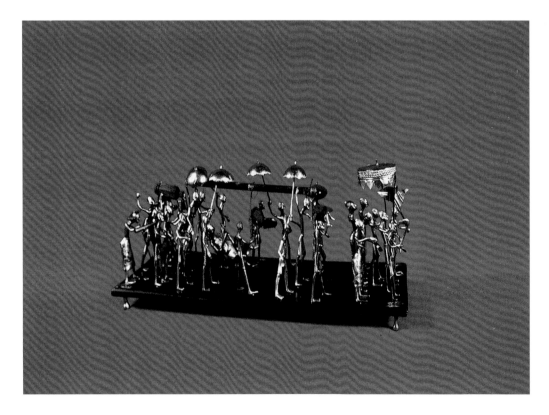

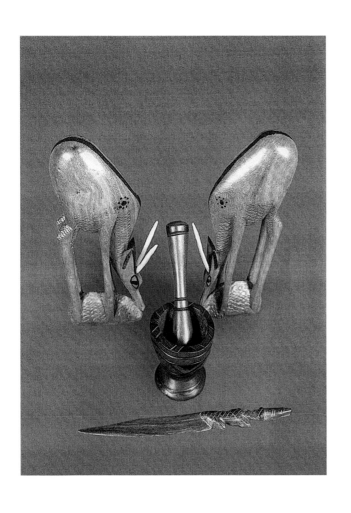

CONFERMENT SOUVENIR ●

Presented to the GREAT LEADER of the Democratic People's
Republic of Korea, President KIM IL SUNG, ANYANWU I (THE SUN OF
UMUOZZI COMMUNITY Enugu Ezike, Enugu State, Nigeria

PRESENTER: CHIEF MATTHIAS OKOYE OMEH, EZINWA I OF
UMUTODO COMMUNITY

Former Commissioner for Agriculture Commerce, Industries and
Technology, Enugu State, and Chairman BLOK CONSULTANTS and
M & M General Merchants.

on 15th of April 1995

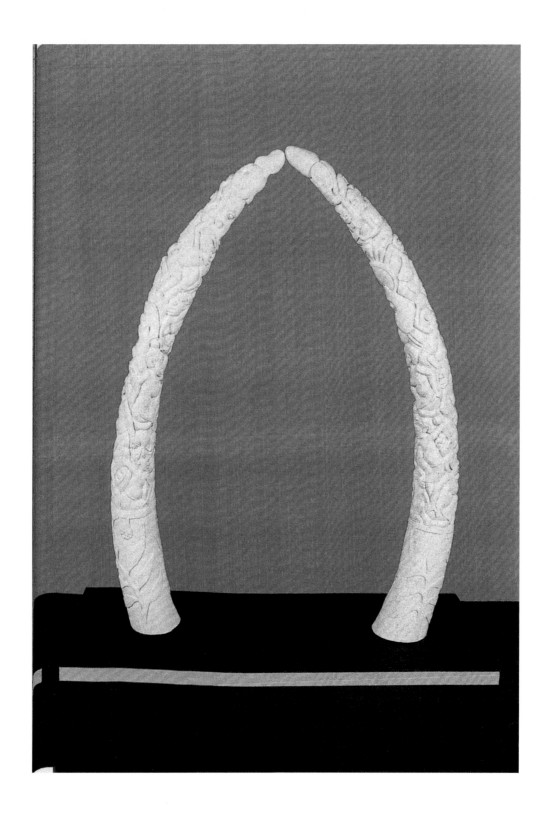

조선의 통일은 그 어떤 외세의 간섭도 없이 평화적으로 이룩되여야 한다

우리는 남조선에 주둔하고있는 모든 외국군대의 철수를 요구한다

미군의 남조선주둔과 조선의 내정에 대한 미국의 간섭은 조선통일의 가장 큰 장애이다

통일은 조선인민 외세의 간섭도 없이 한다고 인정한다

남조선으로부터 외국군대를 철거시킬데 대한 조선인민의 립장을 전적으로 지지한다

조선은 하나이며 절대로 둘로 갈라질수 없다

또고 정부가 남조 도당과 외교관계

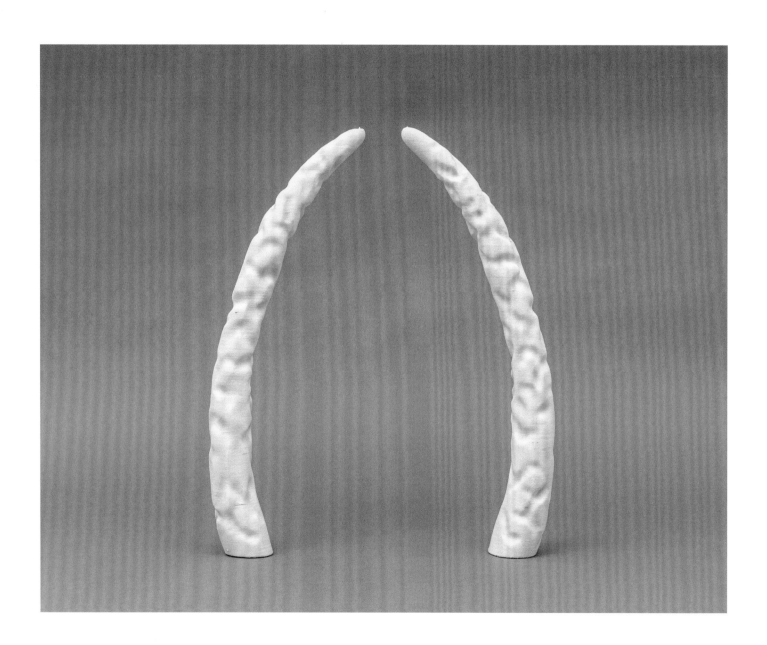

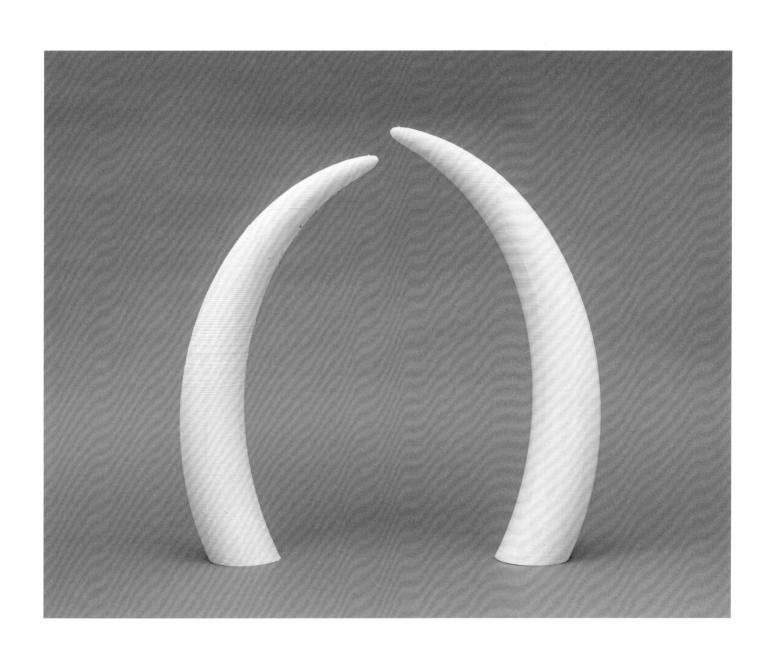

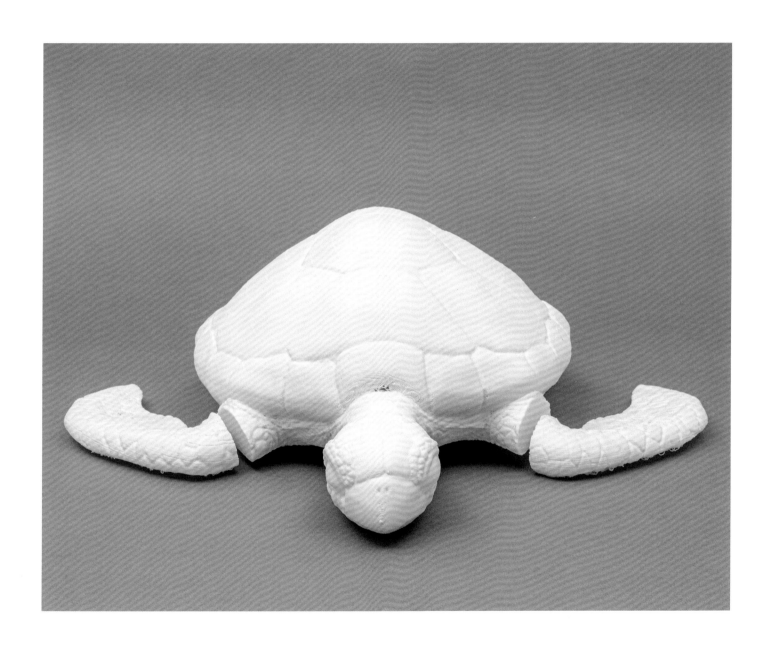

Juche in Africa: North Korea, the Third World, and Non-Alignment in the 1970s[1]

Charles K. Armstrong

Introduction

Few countries in the world have emphasized their distinctiveness and independence as much as the Democratic People's Republic of Korea (DPRK, North Korea). The concept of "Juche," enshrined as the "guiding principle" of North Korean politics for decades, was all about Korea-centrism from the time it was articulated by Kim Il Sung in late 1955: "We are not engaged in any other country's revolution, but solely in the Korean revolution. This, the Korean revolution, determines the essence of Juche in the ideological work of our Party."[2] Yet for a time, roughly from the late 1960s to the mid-1980s, North Korea worked assiduously to present Juche as a model (of politics, economic development, and foreign relations) for other countries to learn from.[3] And indeed, the notion of "self-reliance," as Juche is often translated, resonated with the Zeitgeist in parts of the world freeing themselves from colonial domination in the third quarter of the twentieth century. Yet how could something "uniquely Korean" also be a modelfor export in such far-flung parts of the world, from Asia to Africa to Latin America?

As North Korea's leaders presented their country as an example for the Third World, a number of Third World governments, particularly in Africa, seemed to find aspects of the North Korean model both relevant and attractive. In such countries the idea of self-reliance—and North Korea's apparent success at self-reliant development—held a powerful allure. And Kim Il Sung was not without his admirers among the radical elements in the first world as well. Eldridge Cleaver, an early leader of the Black Panther Party in the United States, wrote from exile in the early 1970s:

In 1969, we went to Korea in search of something we have been seeking all over the world, something for which we have dedicated all of our lives, as have all the oppressed peoples of the world. We found it in Korea [...] One thing the United States lacks is a unified national will, defined, analyzed, formulated, and articulated by a leader of genius. Such a leader is Comrade Kim Il Sung.[4]

Rivalry with the South was one important component of North Korea's Third World diplomacy. For the first fifteen years or so after the two Korean states were established in 1948, North Korea had almost no diplomatic ties outside the socialist bloc and was well behind Seoul in the number of countries recognizing its legitimacy. In the 1960s, North Korea opened diplomatic relations with dozens of new countries, mostly in the Middle East and Africa. But South Korea did the same, and it remained ahead of the North in the diplomatic game. In the 1970s, North Korea apparently decided it would try to close the gap, and eventually reached parity with the South in terms of numbers of countries with which it had diplomatic relations. Among the countries with which the DPRK established diplomatic relations between 1971 and 1980, eleven were in Europe, ten in Latin America and the Caribbean, three in the Middle East, thirteen in the Asia-Pacific, and twenty-seven in Africa.[5] The decade of the 1970s was the peak period of Third World diplomacy by North Korea and the promotion of Juche as a model. The African continent held the largest number of the world's newly independent countries, and North Korean would establish long-lasting and amiable ties with many of them.

Juche Diplomacy, 1955–1975

North Korea's diplomatic relations were confined solely to other socialist states until the late 1950s. In the mid-1950s North Korea began to cultivate ties with political movements and states that were just beginning to be called the "Third World": the developing nations of Asia, African and Latin America that refused to take sides in the Cold War struggle between the US and Soviet-led blocs. Throughout the wave of independence struggles in Africa and Asia during the 1950s to the 1980s, North Korea declared its solidarity with various anti-colonial and national liberation movements. The first non-socialist Third World government with whom

1.
This article is adapted from Chapter 5 of Charles K. Armstrong, *Tyranny of the Weak: North Korea and the World, 1950–1992* (Ithaca, NY: Cornell University Press, 2013).

2.
Kim Il Sung, "On Eliminating Dogmatism and Formalism and Establishing Juche in Ideological Work," *Kim Il Sung Works* vol. 9 (Pyongyang: Foreign Languages Publishing House, 1982), 395.

3.
Jon Halliday, "The North Korean Model: Gaps and Questions," *World Development* vol. 9, no. 9/10 (1981), 889–905.

4.
Eldridge Cleaver, forward to *Juche! The Speeches and Writings of Kim Il Sung*, edited and introduced by Li Yuk-Sa (New York: Grossman Publishers, 1972), ix–x.

5.
Byung-chul Koh, *The Foreign Policy Systems of North and South Korea* (Berkeley: University of California Press, 1984), 148–149.

the DPRK established diplomatic relations was the National Liberation Front of Algeria, in September 1958.[6] A few years earlier, in April 1955, the DPRK had sent a delegation to the Asian Conference for the Relaxation of International Tension (ACRIT) in New Delhi, the first major Third World conference attended by North Koreans. The term "Third World" had itself only recently been coined by the French demographer Alfred Sauvy, to describe the countries that sought to occupy a space independent of the "two worlds" of the US-aligned and pro-Soviet nations. Although North Korea (along with South Korea) was excluded from the 1955 Afro-Asian Conference in Bandung, Indonesia—the event that effectively launched the Non-Aligned Movement (NAM) —the DPRK media covered the Bandung Conference quite positively.[7] When Britain, France and Israel intervened in Egypt to regain Western control of the Suez Canal from Gamal Abdel Nasser's Egyptian government in late 1956, the DPRK publicly supported Egypt in the Suez Crisis, and even sent a small amount of economic assistance to the Nasser government. This was a foretaste of the extensive assistance and advice North Korea would give to Third World governments in future years, especially in Africa.

The warm reception, or at least strong interest, North Korea's diplomatic offensive received in many Third World countries is not difficult to explain. North Korea in the 1960s and 1970s looked like a model of post-colonial nation-building, having been founded by anti-imperialist fighters, built up an impressive industrial economy, and successfully resisted (albeit with considerable Chinese assistance) the military might of the United States in the Korean War. With no foreign troops on its soil after the withdrawal of the Chinese People's Volunteers in 1958, North Korea looked particularly good in contrast to the South, which was heavily dependent on US economic assistance and host to tens of thousands of American troops. Externally, the DPRK propaganda line was consistently in favor of anti-colonial nationalism and independence throughout the Third World. In his frequent commentary on the Juche idea, Kim Il Sung regularly pointed to "US Imperialism" as the main enemy of the Third World peoples, and advocated Juche as the very embodiment of anti-imperialism. The DPRK portrayed the North Koreans' struggle against the US and South

Korea as identical with the struggle of Third-World peoples for independence, and completely compatible with "Proletarian Internationalism":

> We should unite closely with the peoples of all the socialist countries; we should actively support the Asian, African and Latin American peoples struggling to throw off the imperialist yoke, and strengthen solidarity with them.[8]

It was a revolutionary spirit very much in sync with the movements for Third World solidarity in the age of decolonization.

Establishing ties to many new countries in this way raised North Korea's diplomatic profile in the world. The DPRK used its new diplomatic stature to advance its agenda in the United Nations, advocating DPRK participation in General Assembly debates on the Korean Question, an end to US dominance in UN activities on the Korean Peninsula, and the removal of US forces from South Korea. Outside the UN forum, North Korea had some success in playing a leading role in the Non-Aligned Movement that was launched in Belgrade, Yugoslavia in 1961. Trade and military exchange with non-socialist Third World countries benefitted North Korea economically as well, although economic relations with China and the Soviet-bloc states remained far more important to the DPRK throughout the Cold War period. June 1961 was a particularly fruitful month for North Korea's Third World diplomacy: DPRK Trade Minister Yi Chu-yŏn visited Indonesia and India, opening trade and consular relations with these two countries, while also establishing a trade agreement with Burma. On a tour through West Africa that summer, North Korean officials signed similar trade agreements with Guinea, Mali and Ghana. Guinea, in fact, had been the first sub-Saharan African country with which the DPRK established full diplomatic relations, in October 1958 (and only the second non-East bloc country after Algeria, earlier that year). In October 1961, North Korea and Mali produced a joint communiqué on "Afro-Asian solidarity against US imperialism."[9]

In the Middle East, North Korea's first diplomatic success was with the Nasser government of Egypt, to which the DPRK had given token financial assistance

6.
Barry K. Gills, *Korea versus Korea: A Case of Contested Legitimacy* (London: Routledge, 1996), 60.

7.
Chosŏn chungang nyŏngam [Korea Central Yearbook] (Pyongyang, 1955).
8.
Kim Il Sung, *On the Juche Idea* (New York: The Guardian, 1980), 262.

9.
George Ginsburgs and Roy U.T. Kim, *Calendar of Diplomatic Affairs, Democratic People's Republic of Korea, 1945–1975* (Moorestown, NJ: Symposia Press, 1977), 71.

The Gifts from Africa

during the Suez Crisis. In 1961, a DPRK delegation visited Egypt to discuss establishing consular relations, and North Korea sent similar preliminary missions to South Yemen, Morocco, and Iraq. North Korea officially condemned Israeli actions in the Middle East as complicit with US imperialism; the DPRK strongly sided with the Arab states against Israel in the 1967 war, for example. By 1963, the fifteenth anniversary of the founding of the DPRK, North Korea was no longer the isolated outpost of the Soviet bloc that it had been in the aftermath of the Korean War: twenty-two foreign delegations participated in the fifteenth-anniversary celebrations in Pyongyang, representing for the first time many Asian, African and Middle Eastern countries outside the socialist bloc. The following year, Pyongyang hosted the Asian Economic Conference, attended by delegates from thirty-four Asia-Pacific and African countries. Kim Il Sung proclaimed the DPRK a model of self-reliant development and anti-imperialist independence for the entire Third World.[10]

Kim's most important Third World summit appearance of the 1960s was in Indonesia in April 1965, the tenth anniversary of the Bandung Conference. This was Kim's first visit outside the socialist bloc since the founding of the DPRK. Indonesian president Sukarno had visited Pyongyang the previous year, where he seems to have been greatly impressed by both North Korea's self-reliance strategy and Kim Il Sung's leadership. Kim was accompanied in his visit to Indonesia by his son Kim Jong Il, and during this visit Kim Jong Il met Sukarno's daughter Megawati, whom he invited to Pyongyang in 2002, when Megawati was president of Indonesia. In Indonesia as in many parts of the Third World, North Korea's connections would be deep, personal and long-lasting.

The highlight of Kim Il Sung's 1965 visit to Indonesia was his speech at Ali Archam Social Science Institute in Jakarta on April 14. The speech, entitled *On Socialist Construction in the Democratic People's Republic of Korea and the South Korea Revolution*, outlined the basic principles of Juche, demanded the withdrawal of all foreign forces from Korea, and called for strengthening the anti-imperialist movement in Asia, Africa and Latin America. In the middle part of the speech Kim outlines the principles of Juche, making his subsequently famous declaration

that the DPRK is based on "Juche in ideology, independence in politics, self-reliance in economy, self-defense in national defense."[11] This was the first time Kim had so explicitly presented his country as a model for Third World development, and his speech was well-received. Kim was given an honorary degree by the Indonesians and praised effusively by Sukarno. Kim Il Sung had suddenly emerged as a leader of the "non-aligned" countries of the Third World.

North Korea in the Non-Aligned Movement
The year 1975 marked the high point of North Korea's diplomatic offensive in the Third World, and toward the non-aligned countries in particular.[12] In August, the foreign ministers of the member countries of the Non-Aligned Movement agreed to admit the DPRK as a member, while rejecting Seoul's application to join. In the United Nations, Third-World countries generally supported North Korea's position on Korean peninsula issues—for example, in opposing the UN Commission for the Unification and Rehabilitation of Korea (UNCURK), which was dissolved in 1973, the year North and South Korea gained observer status at the UN.[13]

The Third World in general and Africa in particular seemed to be moving in North Korea's direction politically. In a period of some eighteen months in 1974 and 1975, for example, self-professed Marxist-Leninist leaders came to power in Angola, Mozambique, Madagascar and Ethiopia. By the end of the 1970s, a dozen states in Africa could be considered Marxist-Leninist or at least what the Soviets called "socialist-oriented."[14] Many African states welcomed North Korean aid and cooperation of various kinds. Economic exchange took off: between 1957 and 1982, 57% of North Korea's trade agreements were signed with African countries. Military assistance was also substantial; according to one estimate, there were 8,000 North Korean military personnel sent to 38 countries between 1966 and 1983, while in the same period North Korea provided training for some 7,000 military personnel from 30 countries.[15] North Korean engineers and urban planners helped to rebuild cities and construct factories, and North Korean artists built monuments and heroic statues in more than a dozen African countries. While much has changed in Africa, the Korean Peninsula and the world since the

10.
Chosŏn chungang nyŏngam [Korea Central Yearbook] (Pyongyang, 1964), 34–35.
11.
Dae-sook Suh, *Kim Il Sung, the North Korea Leader* (New York: Columbia University Press, 1988), 308.

12.
Samuel S. Kim, "Pyongyang, the Third World and Global Politics," in Tae-hwan Kwak et al., eds. *The Two Koreas in World Politics* (Boulder, CO: Westview, 1984), 73.
13.
See Kim Il Sung, *The Non-Alignment Movement is a Mighty Anti-Imperialist Revolutionary Force of Our Times* (Pyongyang: Foreign Languages Publishing House, 1976).

14.
Ibid., 164.
15.
Young C. Kim, "North Korea and the Third World," in *North Korea in a Regional and Global Context*, ed. Robert A. Scalapino and Hongkoo Lee (Berkeley: University of California Press, 1986), 338.

heyday of North Korea-Africa contacts in the 1970s and 1980s, monumental art is perhaps the most visible and lasting legacy of North Korea's Africa diplomacy today.

North Korea in Africa

Africa was the great prize for North Korea's Third-World diplomacy, both because of the continent's large number of newly independent countries that might be persuaded to confer diplomatic recognition to the DPRK and support North Korea's positions in the UN, as well as its potential as a site for demonstrating North Korea's successful development strategy. Similar to China at the time, North Korea gave economic aid to several African countries on very generous terms.[16] For the new and underdeveloped African regimes, North Korea's success at rapid industrialization, without dependence on Western capital, was impressive. As one pro-Juche African scholar put it, in a book published in the DPRK,

> In the period of industrialization which lasted less than 20 years, a country which had been backward like today's Africa was totally transformed and has been converted into a powerful, independent industrial country which calls forth the admiration of the people of the world.[17]

North Korea put a great deal of energy and resources into demonstrating its popularity as a political and economic model among developing nations. For example, a "Scientific Seminar of the Middle East, Near East and African Countries on the Great Idea of Juche" was held in Mogadishu, Somalia in November 1973.[18] Three years later another "Scientific Seminar on the Juche Idea" was held in Madagascar, presided over by president Didier Ratsiraka himself.[19] All publications regarding these seminars showed attendees unequivocally praising the achievements of the DPRK and eagerly reading the works of Kim Il Sung.

North Korea did not present itself as a model for precise imitation, much less did it attempt to reshape African countries in the image of the DPRK. Rather, North Korea offered assistance in a limited number of sectors—economic, military, and cultural—and offered its own experience as inspiration for a kind of development path that each Third World country would have to find on its own. As Kim Il Sung told the president of the Front for the Liberation of Mozambique (FRELIMO) in May 1975, shortly after the country had gained its independence from Portugal:

> Now I am going to talk about our experience in building a new country... Our experience may not suit the conditions in Mozambique. So I hope that you will take it, to all intents and purposes, as a reference in your construction of a new society.[20]

Most of Kim's speech was a recapitulation of North Korean history in the early post-liberation years. The main "lessons" he offered his Mozambican guests were the need to create a broad-based political party and affiliated mass organizations, instigate "democratic" reforms such as land redistribution, and above all to make sure that the economy was entirely under the command of the state. Following his brief history lesson, Kim offered assistance to Mozambique in areas such as irrigation, farming technology, and the construction of "small local industry factories." Although Kim admitted that "the quality of our goods is still not so high," he offered free aid, including food.[21]

The Case of Ethiopia

Ethiopia under Mengistu Haile Mariam was in some ways the most important of the Marxist-Leninist experiments in Africa. In September 1974 the Derg, a committee of officers in the Ethiopian military, led an overthrow of the government of Emperor Haile Selassie and declared Ethiopia to be a Marxist-Leninist, one-party state. Mengistu became chairman of the junta in 1977. By then Ethiopia had taken a decisive turn toward the Soviet Union, and the Soviets and their allies rewarded Mengistu's regime generously. Ethiopia in the late 1970s and early 1980s represented the most important Soviet-led intervention outside Europe, the largest foreign assistance program the USSR had undertaken since China in the 1950s, and the largest socialist multilateral aid project since the reconstruction of North Korea after the Korean War. Cuba played a particularly active role, sending 11,600 soldiers and 1,000 advisors.[22] Although North Korea gave less assistance to Mengistu's regime than did the USSR, East Germany or Cuba, it was an

16.
For Chinese aid to Africa in the Maoist period, see Philip Snow, *The Star Raft: China's Encounter with Africa* (London: Weidenfeld and Nicolson, 1988), 144–185.

17.
Huber Mono Ndkana, *Revolution and Creation: A Treatise on the Juche Philosophy* (Pyongyang: Foreign Language Publishing House), 229. In the 1970s Pyongyang sponsored a great many books by Third World authors praising the North Korean system and Kim Il Sung's genius behind it. See for example *Comrade Kim Il Sung, an Ingenious Thinker and Theoretician* (Pyongyang: Foreign Languages Publishing House, 1975) and Muhammad al Missuri, *Kim Il Sungism: Theory and Practice* (Pyongyang: Foreign Languages Publishing House, 1978).

18.
The Third World Marches Forward to Independence and Self-Reliance: Documents of the Scientific Seminar of the Middle East, Near East and African Countries on the JUCHE Idea (Beirut: Dar Al-Talie, 1975). Two years later Somalia would switch to a pro-Western position and North Korea would become an ally of Somalia's archrival, Ethiopia.

The Gifts from Africa

important source of aid, advice and expertise for Ethiopia under the Derg.

North Korea's decision to send military advisors, engineers, and agricultural experts was almost a mirror-image of its role as an aid recipient after the Korean War, and perhaps that was a conscious motivation. Just as the Soviets helped rebuild Pyongyang and the East Germans Hamheung, so the North Koreans helped to reconstruct the Ethiopian capital Addis Ababa as a "socialist" metropolis. Architects, urban planners, and engineers helped to redesign parts of the city, both above ground and in infrastructure projects such as the sewer system. Among various artistic and architectural projects, perhaps the most impressive contribution North Koreans made to the Addis Ababa cityscape was the Tiglachin Monument, designed by sculptors of the Mansudae Art Studio and bearing a striking resemblance to the Juche Tower in Pyongyang. North Korean military advisors trained Ethiopian forces in anti-guerilla tactics and for fighting against Somalia, which had been pro-American since 1975. DPRK assistance built two large ammunitions factories in the country and supported Ethiopians' ambitions to produce their own weapons. North Korean agricultural experts helped with land reform and crop production, including an attempt to plant rice in the south of the country that utterly failed. Another distinctive skill the North Koreans had was staging parades and "mass games," which they taught the Ethiopians to perform for the celebration of the tenth anniversary of the Revolution in September 1984.[23]

According to my interviews with Mr. Assefe Medhanie, formerly in charge of foreign affairs for the Ethiopian Workers' Party, the Mengistu regime sought "loose solidarity under the umbrella of the Soviet Union," and turned to several socialist countries for support. The Chinese were not forthcoming with the kind of weaponry and aid they wanted, and the Chinese presence in Ethiopia was minimal. Assefe observed that there appeared to be some competition between the Cubans and North Koreans over military advice to the Ethiopians, but although the Koreans helped in the war against Somalia, the scale of the Cuban assistance—including large numbers of combat troops—was far greater. Assefe had the sense that the North Koreans liked Mengistu, the kind of take-charge "big man" who seemed like a Kim Il Sung in the making. Mengistu himself visited Pyongyang twice, and was deeply impressed by what he saw there, so much so that he made his citizens sport North Korean-style uniforms.[24]

Nevertheless, despite the mutual admiration that existed between the two governments, Juche never really took root in Ethiopia. A few university professors were invited to Pyongyang to study Juche and—as Mr. Assefe told me—"came back running." Some students went to study Taekwondo, but many more students went to Eastern Europe to study modern administration and science; a group of North Korean students also came to study in Addis Ababa. Party relations were good, with members attending each other's Party Congresses. But the deeper "lessons" of the North Korean experience did not seem particularly applicable to the Ethiopian environment. Juche, the Ethiopians felt, was not translatable.[25]

Conclusion

Although the People's Democratic Republic of Ethiopia disappeared in 1991, the DPRK retains many strong ties to Third World nations in general and African countries in particular. North Korea remains an active member of the Non-Aligned Movement, which now includes some 120 countries. Currently NAM is the second-largest organization of states in the world after the United Nations, but still does not include South Korea. Despite decades of wrenching change—the end of the Cold War order, the disintegration of the Soviet Union, the global ascendance of neo-liberalism, economic catastrophe in North Korea and the ongoing confrontation over its nuclear program—the relations cultivated some fifty years ago between North Korea and the Third World have mostly survived. North Korea has had especially close bilateral relations with several African nations, including Tanzania, Madagascar, and Zimbabwe among others. And as the economic gap between rich and poor countries has grown wider in recent decades—including the gap between North and South Korea—North Korea may in some respects belong to the Third World now even more than in the era of decolonization. The legacy of Juche diplomacy survives in North Korea and in much of the Third World, not least in the North Korean-built statues and monuments scattered across the African continent.

19.
Juche: The Banner of Independence (Pyongyang: Foreign Languages Publishing House, 1977).
20.
Kim Il Sung, "Talk to the President of the Liberation Front of Mozambique," in *Kim Il Sung Works* vol. 30 (Pyongyang: Foreign Languages Publishing House, 1987), 119.
21.
Ibid., 139–140.

22.
Odd Arne Westad, *The Global Cold War: Third World Interventions and the Making of Our Times* (Cambridge: Cambridge University Press, 2005), 277, 279.
23.
Donald L. Donham, *Marxist Modern: An Ethnographic History of the Ethiopian Revolution* (Berkeley: University of California Press, 1999), 14. Donham remarks that the Mengistu regime spent US $50 million dollars on the anniversary celebration just as the historic Ethiopian famine was emerging, a famine that would take hundreds of thousands of lives.

24.
Author's interview with Dr. Min Chul Yoo, Addis Ababa, November 30, 2004.
25.
Author's interview with Assefe Medhanie, December 1, 2004.

The African Renaissance does not Have to Look like North Korea

Sean O'Toole

The Democratic People's Republic of Korea, the totalitarian state led by three generations of the Kim family and known in the English-speaking world as North Korea, has been involved in the production of state-sponsored public art and ceremonial monuments across post-colonial Africa for a half century. Given the duration and geographical spread of these projects, it is fair to wonder how influential this imported style of socialist realism has been on art and artists in sub-Saharan Africa. Have large-scale projects like Zimbabwe's National Heroes' Acre (1981), Botswana's Three Dikgosi Monument (2005) or Senegal's African Renaissance Monument (2010) tangibly impacted practice? And what, if anything, does Africa's polymorphous creative class (among them sculptors, painters, architects, curators and critics) think about North Korea's active involvement in the construction of memory on the continent? Che Onejoon's three-channel documentary *Mansudae Master Class* (2013–ongoing) offers substantial hints and clues.

Combining found news material with original footage filmed on location in Africa by the artist, *Mansudae Master Class* presents an expansive historical survey of North Korea's involvement in the construction of public memory in thirteen African states. They include durable democracies like Senegal, which achieved independence from France in 1960, and fragile polities like Zimbabwe, a southern African country that displays the same anti-democratic tendencies as North Korea. As part of his visual research Che interviewed a diverse assembly of protagonists. Some, like Gabonese artist Christian Ndong Menzamet and Senegalese architect Pierre Goudiaby Atepa, have been directly involved in projects with Mansudae Art Studio (founded in 1958) and its export division Mansudae Overseas Projects (founded in 1967). They speak favourably of their collaborations with this commercial art studio and proxy for the North Korean state. Others interviewed by Che are, however, more critical, notably Zimbabwean artist Owen Maseko and

the director general of the Institute of National Museums Paul Bakua-Lufu Badibanga. Their testimonies suggest a more complicated reception of North Korea's projects (Mansudae's projects) in Africa.

Che did not explicitly set out to explore the influence of Mansudae's projects on artistic and museological practice in Africa. In the main, his film *Mansudae Master Class* is occupied with North Korea's shifting motives in relation to its client states. The film does not purposefully examine the impact and effect of North Korea's rococo brand of socialist realism on cultural practices and artistic debates in Africa, which has been substantial. Rather than broadly survey Mansudae's projects and their reception in all thirteen sub-Saharan states where this North Korean studio has been involved, I will focus on Mozambique and Senegal, as well as discuss parallel initiatives in South Africa. Art is an expression of place, and North Korea's nostalgic brand of figurative socialist realism asserts itself in countries with distinctive histories. It is nonetheless hoped that this granular focus on Mozambique, Senegal and South Africa will illuminate broader ideas and attitudes involving memory and the function of art in postcolonial Africa, as well as draw attention to an important attribute of Che's film: *Mansudae Master Class* is an elegant deliberation on the longue durée of the Cold War in Africa.

The arrival of socialist realism in Africa predates the founding of North Korea in 1948. For example, in 1930s South Africa, Johanna and Hester Cornelius, two white Afrikaans-speaking sisters working in the garment industry in Johannesburg, became active in union politics. In 1933, Johanna spent a month in the Soviet Union as a trade union delegate. Both sisters recognised the power of culture in promoting class-consciousness; they both wrote plays, poems and songs lionizing working-class life. In her best-known play, *The Sacrifice* (1941), Hester described the conflicts of a struggling white farmer forced to seek work in the city's gold-mining industry to survive.[1] Małgorzata Drwal, a Polish scholar of South African working-class history, has noted how the play grafts the Soviet aesthetic of socialist realism onto an Afrikaner cultural setting.[2] On the opposite end of the continent, the Egyptian revolution of 1952 ushered in a wave of new realism in literature, including socialist realism, notably through the writing of Marxist critic

1.
Jon Lewis, *Industrialisation and Trade Union Organization in South Africa, 1924–55* (Cambridge, Cambridge University Press, 1984), 73.

Mahmoud Amin El Alem. My point here is that socialist realism is a long-established genre and trope in African arts and letters. Its themes of heroic struggle and solidarity dovetailed with lived experiences and were easily adapted in service of anti-colonial resistance.

Adaptation powerfully features in the story of revolutionary Mozambican art. This East African country's armed struggle for independence from Portugal (1964–1975) culminated in the founding of a one-party state based on Marxist principles led by Samora Machel. Machel maintained strong ties with North Korea, visiting the country twice, in 1975 and 1984. Kim Il Sung, the charismatic founder of North Korea, hailed Mozambique's much-admired first president as a "comrade." Cordial relations between the two communist states were occasionally tested, notably when Machel signed a non-aggression pact with South Africa's white-minority apartheid government in 1984. An incident from the preceding decade is however more instructive in the context of this essay.

In 1978, North Korea gifted a painting to Mozambique's new Museum of the Revolution, located in the state capital Maputo. The painting depicts a jubilant crowd of black Mozambicans greeting a parade of soldiers in olive fatigues led by Machel. The processional theme and heroic style of the painting has precedents in both North Korean and Chinese revolutionary art, but ultimately owes its form to the official art championed by Joseph Stalin after his well-documented purge of the Russian avant-garde in the 1930s. But this is not what upset Machel about the painting. In 1983, it was reported that Machel had been unhappy with the rendering of the eyes of its chief protagonists, which, it was claimed, looked more Korean than African, and had to be significantly retouched.[3] Machel's interest in art and culture as a tool of revolution was sincere and not motivated by personal vanity. In 1977, for instance, French filmmaker Jean-Luc Godard was invited by Machel's government to assist in the establishment of the country's first television station. But it is Machel's involvement in the realignment of Mozambique's indigenous sculpture that is more germane to an appreciation of Che's project.

The American art historian Alex Bortolot has extensively written about Machel's attempts to champion indigenous blackwood sculpture as a primary symbol of Mozambique's socialist project. This distinctive tradition of figurative wood sculpture is linked to Makonde artisans in northern Mozambique. Prior to independence, the principal market was for their wares were European tourists. In 1966, while engaged in his revolutionary insurgency, Machel organized sixty-two Makonde guerrillas, all of them former sculptors, into an artists' cooperative. Machel was attracted to blackwood sculpture, writes Bortolot, because it presented a functioning example of workshop-based artistic creation—a kind of indigenous Mansudae, if you will—that corresponded with the state's ideological model of collective and cooperative production. This state-sponsored art was designed to operate as an analogue to socialist realism; it expanded its vernacular forms, rather than negated its operability in Africa.

Shortly after Mozambique's independence in 1975, during a state visit to North Korea, Machel gifted Kim Il Sung an elaborate cylindrical sculpture in the blackwood style. The work depicts a Portuguese colonial officer stacked upon a Makonde elder. Surrounding this central image of colonial domination is an ensemble of Mozambican soldiers and villagers, their presence declaring the integration of civilian and military resistance to oppression.[4] As part of his long-term exploration of North Korea's involvement in postcolonial Africa, Che tracked down Machel's gift. Titled *Solidarity*, the blackwood sculpture now forms part of the displays in a large museum complex known as the International Friendship Exhibition in Myohyangsan (Mt. Myohyang), North Korea. Che did not directly encounter the object: although possible to travel to North Korea, it is difficult for South Koreans to obtain an entry visa. Instead, Che visited a North Korean library in Seoul where he obtained a catalogue documenting the International Friendship Exhibition's holdings of more than 224,000 gifts from 179 countries. His archival project *International Friendship: The Gifts from Africa* (2017–2018) includes a reproduction of Machel's gift that the artist illicitly scanned from the catalogue.

Machel's ambitious experiment with cultivating an indigenous socialist realism, an experiment that alloyed a local idiom to the global idea of heroic socialism, ultimately failed. The Mozambican state was unable to sustain production levels matching those of the former colonial trade. Makonde artisans drifted into other forms

2.
Małgorzata Drwal, "Afrikaans Working-Class Drama in the Early 1940s: Socialist Realism in *Die Offerande* by Hester Cornelius," *Dutch Crossing* (2020).

3.
Joseph Lelyveld, "The Talk of Maputo; Amid Grinding Shortages, A Party in Mozambique," *New York Times*, October 8, 1983.

4.
Alexander Bortolot, "Artesãos da Nossa Pátria: Makonde Blackwood Sculptors, Cooperatives, and the Art of Socialist Revolution in Post-Colonial Mozambique," *Field*, Issue 6 (Winter 2017): http://field-journal.com/issue-6/artesaos-da-nossa-patria-makonde-blackwood-sculptors-cooperatives-and-the-art-of-socialist-revolution-in-post-colonial-mozambique.

of individualized sculpture, notably producing masks for local clients. One measure of the failure of Machel's idealistic project is a nine-metre bronze statue of this African liberation leader situated on Independence Square in Maputo. The sculpture portrays Machel in military fatigues pointing his index finger to the future. Unveiled in 2011, the statue was designed and constructed in Pyongyang. It ignores notions of entanglement and collectivity central to the ujamaa-style of blackwood sculpture gifted to Kim Il Sung, offering instead a singular and superhuman figure. The bronze announces the triumph of the big man. This idea is central to many Mansudae's projects, including the bronze likeness of Gabonese dictator Omar Bongo erected in Franceville in the 1980s and documented by Che in 2015. As a visual proposition the big man on a plinth is emblematic not only of the Kim family's needs and aspirations, but also speaks to the vanities and follies of Africa's postcolonial elites.

The outsize form of the Machel sculpture on Maputo's Independence Square chimes with similar projects in Senegal and South Africa. In 2010, Senegal's president Abdoulaye Wade inaugurated a nearly 50-metre tall bronze statue of an idealized black African family, their gaze directed west over the Atlantic Ocean. Installed on a northern coastal road of the capital Dakar, the monument is a projective symbol in the mould of New York's Statue of Liberty. At its unveiling Wade described the North Korean-made sculpture as a symbol of a continent freed from "several centuries of imprisonment in the abyssal depths of ignorance, intolerance and racism."[5]

Senegalese architect Pierre Goudiaby Atepa is often credited as the monument's designer. In fact, Virgil Magherusan, a Romanian-born figurative sculptor, designed the bronze centrepiece, with fabrication handled by Mansudae. The monument was a long-cherished ideal of Wade. Ery Camara, an influential Senegalese-born art critic and curator linked to the country's first president, Léopold Senghor, briefly advised Wade on the project. Camara told me that local sculptor Ousmane Sow, well known internationally for his large and expressive bronzes portraying black figures in valiant and athletic poses, had offered Wade a suitable work from his studio for the proposed monument.

"The African renaissance does not have to look like North Korea," Camara counselled Wade. The president rejected this advice, as well as Sow's sculpture. "I can do whatever I want," the president told Camara.[6]

Senegal's African Renaissance Monument has been widely criticized since its unveiling. High-profile critics include N'Goné Fall and Simon Njami, both internationally established curators working between Africa and Europe. Fall wrote a satirical article about the monument for the pan-African literary journal The Chronic, while Njami told me, "We are sick of all those old people thinking old things in old terms." Njami is not against a monument paying tribute to Africa's post-independence transformation—"Why not?"—but describes the project signed-off by Wade as the "most outrageously stupid thing in the world".[7] Controversial it may well be, but Dakar's jutting monument is also widely loved. It is popular with day-trippers. Che's *International Friendship* includes portraits of smiling visitors from Burkina Faso, Congo, Ethiopia and Mauritania. Che collected these photos from street photographers near the monument and has included them in his archive to show the positive acceptance of the African Renaissance Monument.

It is not only tourists who have been inspired by the monument. In late 2010, Dakar hosted the third edition of the World Festival of Negro Arts (FESMAN) with a thematic focus on the African renaissance. Among the invited artists was South African sculptor and textile artist Mary Sibande. The artist is best known for her costumed black female character Sophie, who is equal parts post-apartheid superhero and alter ego for the artist's mother and grandmother, both of whom laboured as domestic servants in white homes in apartheid South Africa. Sibande, whose work was featured in the Venice Biennale 2011 (Fig. 1), was greatly impressed by Dakar's new monument. "It is romantic and I think that romance is often missing or misinterpreted when thinking of the images from Africa," Sibande told me. "As a public image it is descriptive, allowing viewers from all walks of life to engage with the simple idea."[8] The monument was not closed-off from its public, she added, its meaning and reception not confined to a group educated in the codes of visual culture.

Sibande's generous reception of the African Renaissance Monument offers a useful entrée into changing attitudes to figuration—especially black figuration—in

5.
"Protests cloud opening of Wade's 'African Renaissance' statue," *France 24*, April 3, 2010. https://www.france24.com/en/20100403-protests-cloud-opening-wades-african-renaissance-statue.

6.
Author's interview with Ery Camara, Oaxaca, Mexico, November 10, 2018.

7.
Sean O'Toole, "Made in Pyongyang," *Frieze*, Issue 147 (2012). https://www.frieze.com/article/made-pyongyang.

8.
Author's email interview with Mary Sibande, March 27, 2015.

Fig. 1
Installation view of Mary Sibande's *Lovers in Tango*, 2011, South African Pavilion, Venice Biennale 2011, Venice, Italy.
Photo: Sean O'Toole

Fig. 2
Installation view of Long March to Freedom procession, 2018, Groenkloof Nature Reserve, Pretoria, South Africa.
Photo: Sean O'Toole

Fig. 3
Installation view of Long March to Freedom procession, 2015, Oliewenhuis Art Museum, Bloemfontein, South Africa.
Photo: Sean O'Toole

Fig. 4
Jane Alexander, *African Adventure*, 1999–2002, Mixed media, Dimensions variable. Copyright: artist and Tate Collection, London

Fig. 5
Gerard Moerdyk (architect), Voortrekker Monument, 1949, Pretoria, South Africa. Photo: Sean O'Toole

Fig. 6
Artworks portraying white political leaders now stored in Heritage Centre at the Voortrekker Monument, Pretoria, South Africa.
Photo: Sean O'Toole

the contemporary art world, particularly in the wake of social movements like Black Lives Matter and Rhodes Must Fall. The politics of memory in Africa dovetails with these wider attitudes towards blackness in a globalised world. At the same time, monuments are exercises in statecraft. Progressive ideas are frequently mediated by "old people thinking old things in old terms," to quote Njami. This is especially true of South Africa, a country with a North Korean-like zeal for monumentalising big men in stone and bronze.

Up until 1994, many of South Africa's monuments, memorials and public sculptures—most of them conceived and fabricated in the country—celebrated white achievement. The 1994 transfer of power to Nelson Mandela's African National Congress (ANC) party was followed by a brief and highly selective flurry of statue removals, as well as the haphazard production of new landscaped follies, notably Freedom Park (2004) in Pretoria. The maturing of a younger generation of black citizens, born into freedom and frustrated by a lack of transformation, has heralded more robust debate and action. In 2015, following a month-long siege by students, sculptor Marion Walgate's 1934 study of colonial politician and plutocrat Cecil John Rhodes was removed from its plinth at the University of Cape Town. This highly publicised event inspired a national wave of iconoclasm. Sculptor Anton van Wouw's bronze of Boer president Paul Kruger in Pretoria was splashed with lime green paint and has since been fenced off. In 2020, J.M. Swan's bust of Rhodes at his mausoleum in Cape Town, known as Rhodes Memorial (1912), was decapitated.

These acts of destruction coincided with nationalistic production of new sculptures portraying black political leaders. Unlike in Mozambique or Senegal, South Africa's government did not look to Mansudae for assistance. Instead, it has drawn on local resources. One of the principal architects of the new statuary is media personality and businessman Dali Tambo. In 2012, at the ANC's party conference in Bloemfontein, Tambo organised a display of eighteen life-size bronze figures depicting veteran party figures and guerrillas involved in the struggle for liberation. Produced by white artists versed in western sculptural traditions, the heroic poses of the individual figures nonetheless conformed to work by Mansudae's artists. The bronzes were well received by the ruling party

and Tambo was able to secure state support. Over time their number has grown to 100 figures. Arranged in a processional form (Figs. 2 & 3), Tambo's Long March to Freedom bronzes, as they are collectively known, have also been exhibited in Pretoria and Cape Town.

The collective arrangement of figures is a popular trope in contemporary South African art and has been used by prominent artists such as Sibande, Jane Alexander and William Kentridge. (Fig. 4) Tambo's bronzes productively seize on this idea, albeit for monumental purposes. But his procession is also an important publicity tool for Tambo's ambitious project to create a National Heritage Monument in the country's administrative capital, Pretoria, near a key white nationalist landmark known as the Voortrekker Monument. (Figs. 5 & 6) An influential cultural apparatchik, Tambo is the son of former ANC president O.R. Tambo and chief executive of a private company specialising in heritage projects. His portfolio of completed projects shares in the ambition, style and big-man ethos of Mansudae's projects. Notable projects by Tambo's company Koketso Growth include a nine-metre bronze of Nelson Mandela outside the main government building in Pretoria (2013), a similarly large bronze depicting Tambo's father at Johannesburg's main airport (2020), as well as a six-metre monumental bronze of Mandela in Ramallah, Palestine (2016).

Tambo has studiously avoided mentioning Mansudae's place-making exercises in neighbouring countries like Mozambique, Namibia and Zimbabwe—all of them documented by Che—during his flurry of public relations. Instead, he has likened his proposed monument to initiatives in Washington D.C. For Tambo, history, culture and entertainment are closely linked. In 2014 he told a journalist, "Heritage is the show business of history, and I am into show business."[9] Unstated in his laissez-faire account of things is the role of political fealty and creative compromise: Tambo's fledgling projects rely on close links to political power. The need to honour collective memory (of humiliation, struggle and triumph) overlaps with other transactional motives and agendas. In this his projects are both sincere and cynical, much like the multi-decade output of Mansudae. This contradiction is central to an appreciation of Che's *Mansudae Master Class*, a film about the complicated realpolitik informing

9.
Matthew Partridge's interview with Dali Tambo, April 2014.

The Gifts from Africa

North Korea's involvement in the construction of memory in postcolonial Africa.

As should be evident from this abbreviated survey, North Korea is unavoidably implicated in the narrative of artistic practices on the African continent. Whether the project initiated by Kim Jong Il and made possible by the skill of thousands of North Korean art-workers will exert a lasting influence of artistic practice on the African continent remains debatable. It is a moot point, one Che's film does not aim to address. *Mansudae Master Class* broadly anatomises the Kim dynasty's resolute determination to be the chief supplier of graven images to African states intent on memorialising—in bronze and stone—their struggles for independence from European overlords. It shows how Kim Il Sung's project of exporting memorial art and infrastructure merged socialist amity with influence peddling.

The testimony of Yŏng-hwan Ko [Koh Young-hwan], a former North Korean diplomat to central African countries, reveals how North Korea's current ruler, Kim Jong Un, has maintained his grandfather's project, partly out of ideological faith in the country's "Juche" style of socialism, but increasingly for profit, to shore up this so-called hermit kingdom's meagre coffers. Time is central to an appreciation of *Mansudae Master Class*. In his commitment to tracking the workings of a determined political project over a half-century, Che has succeeded in, among other outcomes, presenting a compelling statement on the longue durée of the Cold War.

The Cold War is typically narrated as an ideological deadlock that defined the temperament and arc of global politics throughout the second half of the twentieth century. Prompted by geopolitical tensions between the Soviet Union and the United States, it coincided with the communist revolutions in China and on the Korean peninsula, and decolonisation in Africa. A competition for influence and advantage by northern superpowers, the Cold War played itself out on many fronts, including the cultural sphere where the meaning and function of art was vigorously contested. The public art and ceremonial monuments erected by Mansudae and its affiliates rehearse many of the dogmas of socialist realism, a style ushered in by Stalin's anti-modernist project of celebrating proletarian struggle using classical motifs and proportions.

"The goal was to give to the image of the future world, where all the facts would be the facts of socialist life, a kind of photographic quality, which would make this image visually credible," writes Boris Groys, a German philosopher and well-known historian of Soviet art. "Socialist realism had to be realist only in form and not in content."[10] Machel understood this, and attempted to materialise this ideal in blackwood sculpture. In a recent essay exploring the genealogy and development of the conflict between western and Soviet concepts of art before and during the Cold War, Groys has argued that we still inhabit an "artistic situation" informed by the Cold War.[11] Che's film yields abundant evidence of the endurance of this on-going situation, in Africa, where debates around on-going struggle and exploitation dovetail with public discourse around monuments and memory.

Monuments are powerful statements in remembering. This is why they are so attractive to the state. At their most instrumental, they can be top-down exercises in remembering. But memory exceeds the machinations of the state, any state, in particular the multiple agendas that drive public projects. In 2016, for example, the Namibian government, an important client of Mansudae, confirmed that North Korea had erected an arms and ammunition factory within its borders. Struggle and memory are divisible from the expediencies of politicians, and the building of bronze and stone monuments celebrating their memory. Where monuments are sedentary and unchangeable, always on the cusp of being forgotten, memory flows like a river.

Che's film *Mansudae Master Class* is a reminder of the urgencies of remembering, in particular the hierarchy of forces that led to the creation of postcolonial Africa's eccentric state-sponsored public art and ceremonial monuments. In his 1960 essay on the longue durée as a conceptual tool for historical analysis, French historian Fernand Braudel proposed that to understand the world, "one has to determine the hierarchy of forces, currents and individual movements, and then put them together to form an overall constellation."[12] Methodologically speaking, this is precisely what Che has done in his film *Mansudae Master Class*. The outcome is a compelling study of the meaning of memory in the face of geopolitical manoeuvring by North Korea and the political vanities of post-colonial Africa's ruling elites.

10.
Boris Groys, *Art Power* (Cambridge, Massachusetts, The MIT Press, 2008), 145.

11.
Boris Groys, "The Cold War between the Medium and the Message: Western Modernism vs. Socialist Realism," *e-flux Journal*, no. 104 (November 2019). https://www.e-flux.com/journal/104/297103/the-cold-war-between-the-medium-and-the-message-western-modernism-vs-socialist-realism.

12.
Fernand Braudel, "History and the Social Sciences: The Longue Durée," *Review-Fernand Braudel Center for the Study of Economies, Historical Systems, and Civilizations* 32, no. 2 (2009), 182.

Far Away from the Fatherland: North Korea's Africa Experience in the (Post-) Cold War Era

Chang Joon Ok

Two Monuments in Addis Ababa

There are two monuments related to the Korean Peninsula in Addis Ababa, the capital of Ethiopia. One, the Monument for the Participation of Ethiopia in the Korean War, was erected in 2006 to commemorate that nation's sacrifice in the Korean War. Ethiopia dispatched the Kagnew Battalions to Korea during the Korean War as a member of the United Nations Forces. This monument reflects the diplomatic relationship between the current Ethiopian regime and South Korea. However, there is another monument, called the Tiglachin, meaning "our struggle," which was erected in 1984.

The Tiglachin Monument resembles the Juche Tower erected in Pyongyang in 1982. They look similar because North Korean sculptors built both. The monument commemorates the internationalist solidarity between Cuba and Ethiopia, who fought together against an invasion by Somalia during the Ogaden War (1977–1978). A wall relief shows the Ethiopian revolution led by Mengistu Haile Mariam. The North Korean artists built the Tiglachin Monument to show off the African leader's achievement and his revolutionary experience to the Ethiopian people.

Che Onejoon's documentary project *Mansudae Master Class* (2013–ongoing) examines the trajectory of the North Korean statues, monuments and buildings in Africa produced by the Mansudae Overseas Project Group of Companies, which manages North Korean art activities overseas. Che's work captures the historical relationship between North Korea and Africa.[1]

This article briefly examines the historical context of how North Korea was able to become a close ally to Africa in the 1980s. Using a novel based on a true story that portrays this period and re-edited North Korean archival film footage by Che, I will analyze how North Korea has presented itself to Africa. First, let's take a look at 1975.[2]

Far Away from the Fatherland

The year 1975 was a significant one for North Korea. From April to June of that year, Kim Il Sung visited Romania, Algeria, Mauritania, Bulgaria, and Yugoslavia. Algeria and Mauritania in northwest Africa were the first two stops on his tour. In June, after Africa, Kim traveled to Yugoslavia to meet Tito at a meeting of the Non-Aligned Movement (NAM). From that time on, North Korea took active steps toward joining the NAM. Due to those diplomatic efforts, its application for membership was unanimously approved by the Ministers of Foreign Affairs at the Lima NAM meeting held in Peru in August 1975. In the 1980s, North Korea was an active participant, hosting its first NAM conference in August 1981. The meeting was the 20th anniversary of the founding of the movement. At the conference's conclusion, the participating countries adopted the Pyongyang Declaration: A Non-Aligned Common Food Strategy.

The member states gathered at the conference agreed that the current state of instability in food and agricultural products lay in the international economic system based on social inequality and exploitation held over from colonialism. The ultimate way to overcome this was self-sufficiency in food production. The Pyongyang Declaration suggested concrete action plans at the national level for self-sufficiency in food production. Also, it suggested international cooperation and solidarity between NAM members and other developing countries.[3]

At the conclusion of this meeting, Kim Il Sung pointed out that practical application is just as important as adopting a promising declaration. He also suggested establishing agricultural research institutes in Guinea in West Africa and Tanzania in East Africa, and the creation of model farms within them to test various methods according to each country's situation.[4]

North Korea, which was proud of its own self-sufficient economic model, insisted that the Non-Aligned Movement would be sustainable only when its agricultural sector became self-sufficient. By spreading this message to Africa, they tried to exert their influence on the continent. The cases of Guinea and Tanzania later became a historical example of the relationship between North Korea and Africa more broadly.

1.
Che Onejoon, "A Monumental Journey: Monuments to North Korea in Africa," *Journal of Peace and Unification Studies* 8, no. 2 (2016); Che Onejoon, "*Mansudae Master Class*: North Korean Art in Africa," *Munhwa Kwahak* 96 (2018). http://moonkwa.jinbo.net.

2.
The following is a summary of some of the contents of Chang Joon Ok, "Pyongyang Declarations: Imaginative Geography of North Korea during the Cold War," *Journal of Peace and Unification Studies* 12, no. 1 (2020).
3.
Rodong Sinmun, September 1, 1981.

4.
Kim Il Sung, "Ap'ŭrik'anaradŭl ŭi nongŏp palchŏn ŭl wihayŏ: shingnyang min nongŏp chŭngsan-e kwanhan ppŭllŏkpulgadam min kit'a palchŏn-dosang naradŭl ŭi t'oronhoe-e ch'amgahan tongsŏ ap'ŭrik'anara nongŏp pujang hyŏbŭihoe-esŏ han yŏnsŏl (August 31, 1981)" [For the Development of Agriculture in African Countries: A speech at the East-West African Country Agriculture Ministers' Council which participated in discussions on food

A novel based on a true story about the North Korean agricultural scientific research team dispatched to Guinea was recently published in North Korea.[5] It tells the story of a person who founded the Kim Il Sung Institute of Agricultural Science in 1982 in Kindia Prefecture, about 100 km from Conakry, the capital of Guinea. This book demonstrates the solidarity between North Korea and Africa, and serves as a vivid document showing how the former remembers (or wants to remember) their influence on the latter. In the novel, Kim Kye-hyŏn, the head of the field research team, explains that the reason for the North Korean dispatch of agricultural engineers to Guinea was not merely for economic exchange, but to solve the food problem in Africa independently. Solving it is "key to achieving self-sufficient economy and protecting the people and the nation's independence."[6]

Following the Pyongyang Declaration in 1981 and the proposal by Kim Il Sung, preparations and consultations at the practical level were completed for the investigation team to go to Guinea in November 1981.[7] In December, an investigation team led by Kim Kye-hyŏn was dispatched to Guinea. Two organizations attempt to prevent the mission of the North Koreans.[8] They are an American espionage organization and a Korean version of the same, the latter operating from the Korean Cultural Center in Sierra Leone, neighboring Guinea. They were concerned about the growing North Korean activity in Guinea and the potential global political impact of the Institute of Agricultural Science.

Chosŏn (North Korea) has built the vast Organization of African Unity summit conference hall, drawing the world's attention. Now, they are going to build the Institute of Agricultural Science. It means that Guinea will become a country like Chosŏn, Chosŏn!

So is this a simple matter? Chosŏn is going to build the Institute of Agricultural Science in Guinea. And they are going to build laboratories in neighboring countries. Although new farming methods will be introduced, which will increase food production, their ideology will also be brought to Africa. If Chosŏn's influence rises in East and West Africa like this, our African policy could be broken.[9]

In the novel, the United States and South Korean agents were troubled by North Korean influence in Africa. If African countries followed the North Korean path of independence, self-reliance, and self-defense, the United States and other Western countries would be expelled from the African continent, losing access to its plentiful labor and material resources.[10]

In real life, Guinea's agricultural officials, led by Behanzin Senainon, attended the Pyongyang Conference in August 1981. Afterwards, the deeply impressed Guinean officials energetically promoted the Institute of Agricultural Science.[11] Although the elites of Guinea, under the influence of Western countries, tried to interfere with them, the Guinean government and North Korean agricultural workers agreed to set up the Institute of Agricultural Science in Kilissi, a small village in the prefecture of Kindia. They succeeded in securing a site. And on January 13, 1982, the Kim Il Sung Institute of Agricultural Science was founded, named after Kim Il Sung.

What kind of activities did this institute carry out in Guinea? Workers were dispatched to Africa to teach the Guinean people farming methods appropriate to their country's situation.

The Juche farming method can be good in Asian countries, where the climatic conditions and the large population are similar to that of our country. However, it may be different in African countries. Therefore, it is necessary to research farming methods suitable for Guinea's situation and teach it to the people of that country. The Agricultural Science workers in Tanzania should also research how to improve farming and teach the people of that country.[12]

In the novel, the North Korean workers in Guinea worked hard to present themselves as revolutionary intellectuals of the "Juche" ideology. In the eyes of the residents of Kilissi village, this was a genuine marvel. The North Korean workers were respected. At the same time, people were concerned for their sake and sympathized with them.

The villagers asked them questions, such as: "How much do the Korean agricultural scientists get paid here? If they work under such bad conditions, they should be

and agricultural production and other developing countries (August 31, 1981)], in *Kim Il Sung Complete Works,* vol. 74 (Pyongyang: Workers' Party of Korea Publishing House, 2008), 136–137.

5.
Paek Man-dŭk, *Choguk-ŭl ttŏna mŏn kos-esŏ* [*Far Away from the Fatherland*] (Pyongyang: Munhak yesul ch'ulp'ansa, 2018).

6.
Ibid, 3.

7.
Kim Il Sung, "Kine-wa t'anjinia-e chojik'anŭn nongŏp kwahak yŏn'guso-e p'agyŏnhal ilgundŭl-gwa han tamhwa (November 9, 1981)" [A conversation with the workers to be dispatched to the Agricultural Science Research Institutes in Guinea and Tanzania] in *Kim Il Sung Complete Works* vol. 74 (Pyongyang: Workers' Party of Korea Publishing House, 2008).

8.
Kim Kye-hyŏn in the novel is a character modeled after a real Kye-hyŏn Kim (金桂賢), who studied in Moscow in 1948, served as the director of the Academy of Agricultural Sciences in 1963, and in that capacity visited Guinea in November 1981. *The Biographical Dictionary of North Korean* (Seoul: Chungang ilbosa, 1983), 35.

9.
Paek, 41–42.

10.
Ibid, 57.

11.
Ibid, 26–30.

properly compensated, right?" To this, Paek Jin-sŏk, a member of the Kim Il Sung Institute of Agricultural Science, answers as follows:

> We are not here to make money, but to help Africans. That's why we don't ask a lot of money as others do... The village may or may not know us well. Our revolutionary ancestors, the anti-Japanese partisans, endured even more difficult conditions and fought to beat the Japanese invaders. Our great leader Kim Il Sung hopes that we will live and work with the spirit of the anti-Japanese partisans. Such a thing is unthinkable for European scientists.[13]

Contrary to expectations, North Korean workers' bad working conditions become a springboard for them to exert their "revolutionary spirit." Paek Jin-sŏk enthusiastically told the young North Korean workers at the institute about what it meant to sincerely help Guinea's people: It meant helping the people of Guinea to be self-sufficient.

> The Great Leader Kim said that the way we help Africa is fundamentally different from how capitalist countries help Africa. The capitalist countries only pretend to help African countries, but in reality have them work to make profits for them. However, the Great Leader said that we are genuinely helping Africans by teaching them how to survive independently. That's why we came here to build the Institute of Agricultural Science and study agricultural methods suitable for Guinea's situation to increase agricultural production. We help other neighboring countries so that all African countries can increase their agricultural production.[14]

Following this, Paek Jin-sŏk comments that if the European capitalist countries catch fish for Africans, North Korea teaches them "how to catch fish." He says that imperialist countries continue to exploit other developing nations. Through severely unequal exchanges and unfair trades, capitalist countries produce finished industrial products while developing countries are supposed to produce only raw materials and semi-finished products. Capitalist countries are exploiting and plundering developing countries through this unfair division of labor.[15]

In that case, the only alternative for developing countries was not to be part of the international labor division. And they needed to build a self-sufficient national economy. In order to do this, they had to solve the agricultural problem first. With this as a basis, they could develop other industries. What was more important than any declaration was the construction of a self-sufficient state. To do this, they needed to oppose the imperialist invaders and unfair trade. And it was essential to eliminate the vestiges of colonialism and bring about the unity of the nation and people.

This unity and the pursuit of independence were not necessarily contradictory, because maintaining independence did not necessarily mean refusing to collaborate. The collaboration they had to avoid was that of the imperialist and postcolonial states. The Kim Il Sung Institute of Agricultural Science was a symbol of constructive cooperation among small developing countries.

North Korea in the World, the World in North Korea

As depicted in *Far Away from the Fatherland*, the core of North Korea's activities in Africa was the construction of a "self-reliant" economy. In this way, the Cold War's Western hegemony was closely linked to political meanings and economic issues. The most significant factor shared in common by countries in Asia and Africa that achieved independence during the Cold War and Latin American countries that gained political independence in the early post-War era was economic independence. North Korea was proud of its own experience in building a self-sufficient economy. Based on this experience, North Korea's activities during the Cold War could be positively received globally. This can be seen as the globalization of North Korea.

Interestingly, North Korea's "globalization" was possible because North Korea's independent economic line could be attractive in other developing countries, including Africa. North Korea was envied by many other postcolonial leaders for reviving itself and building an independent state. This is clearly shown in the images of North Korea seen in *All the People Praise Kim Jong Il*[16] and

12.
Kim Il Sung, "Kine-ŭi kimilsŏng nongŏp kwahak yŏn'guso-e kainnŭn nongŏp kwahak ilgundŭlgwa han tamhwa (February 21, 1983)" [A conversation with agricultural science workers at the Kim Il-sung Agricultural Science Research Institute in Guinea (February 21, 1983)] in *Kim Il Sung Complete Works* vol. 77 (Pyongyang: Workers' Party of Korea Publishing House, 2008), 132–133.

13.
Ibid, 198–199.
14.
Ibid, 355–356.
15.
Ibid, 357.

16.
Che Onejoon, *All the People Praise Kim Jong Il* (2017). This film is a re-editing of the original *Manmin-ŭi ch'ingsong* [*All the People Praise Kim Jong Il*] (Pyongyang: Chosŏn girok yŏnghwa ch'waryŏngso, 1992). All references in this article refer to the re-editing.

Worldwide Support for Kim Il Sung[17] edited by Che One-joon. (Fig. 1) The North Korean filmmakers of Chosŏn girok yŏnghwa ch'waryŏngso [the Korean documentary film studio] visited countries around the world and conducted interviews to make *All the People Praise Kim Jong Il* (1992). Through this film, they wanted to capture the outstanding leadership of Kim Il Sung and Kim Jong Il. Che re-edited this film to focus on the experiences of the African region.

The two regions of Africa featured in the film are located in Tanzania and Guinea, where North Korea established the Institute of Agricultural Science in the 1980s (in Tanzania, the Chollima Institute of Agricultural Science was established). When the filmmakers arrived in Guinea's capital Conakry in 1991, they attended a discussion on building an independent Africa. The Guineans thought that the only way to build a new Africa was to establish the Juche ideology. And they said, "Our socialism centered on the masses shall not perish."

In the context of 1991, it is necessary to consider the meaning of the phrase "our style socialism is inevitably unbeatable." In the 1980s, North Korea was an active player in Africa. However, in 1989, the Berlin Wall collapsed, and in 1991 the Soviet Union was also on the verge of dissolution. The Cold War was often defined as a confrontation between US-led allies and Soviet-led allies. This conflict was nearing its end by 1991.

However, from North Korea's point of view, the self-sufficiency and independence that it had been pursuing for a long time became more realizable in 1991. During the Cold War, central powers like the Soviet Union controlled other smaller countries. However, after the Soviet Union's demise, other small countries rejected dogmatism, toadyism, and domination by the Soviet Union. They had to make their revolution independently and creatively.

The post-Cold War era was the first time in history that developing countries opposed being under foreign domination and subjugation and sought self-governance in world politics.[18] In that sense, North Korea's activities in Africa in the 1980s became the ground for Africa's independence. North Korean filmmakers recorded local voices by filming the Juche Agricultural Research Group organized on the far and remote African continent. The Chairman of the Research Group responded, "The Guinean people know the value of North Korean socialism and also learn the Juche ideology that can bring about such a good system."

This scene, from a South Korean point of view now, may seem like some kind of regime-level propaganda in praise of North Korea. However, the Juche Agricultural Research Group was formed in August 1987 and was active in Guinea. Juche agriculture was able to "solve the difficult food problem of Guinea and other African countries." Many Africans actively wanted to learn from the method.[19] Members of the research group studied and discussed the works of Kim Il Sung and Kim Jong Il translated into their languages and tried to solve the real problems they faced. North Korean socialism was perceived as a kind of "good system" to them. The Juche ideology was the philosophical foundation that made such a good system possible. "In Guinea and Tanzania, the Institute for Agricultural Science were built. As our agricultural scientists and technicians were dispatched to other African countries to farm, a whole ideological shift began to occur in African countries. Every time the wasteland was transformed into new arable land, the idea of having to seek the help of the West gradually disappeared. Whenever seeds were sown in the field, the spirit of self-sufficiency was planted in their heads."[20]

As of 1992, the voices of the Guinean people had a special meaning. However, North Korea, labeled by the Guinean people a "good society," suffered a crisis as it went through its "Arduous March" of the 1990s and the death of Kim Il Sung. From the perspective of North Korea, now focused more on the survival of their own regime, it was not easy to maintain a consistent investment in other regions.

In 2012, *Our Leader Praises All the People*, a documentary film commemorating the 100th anniversary of Kim Il Sung's birth, was released. It shows several foreign politicians Kim met in North Korea and abroad during his lifetime. It features leaders of communist countries such as Stalin, Mao Zedong, Zhou Enlai, and Ho Chi Minh. And it includes leaders from Asian countries such as Sukarno and Norodom Sihanouk and leaders from Non-Aligned Movement countries such as Tito. Leaders of African countries also appear frequently.

They expressed their gratitude for the economic, technical, and cultural support that Kim Il Sung gave

17.
Che Onejoon, *Worldwide Support for Kim Il Sung* (2017). This film is a re-editing of the original *Manmini urŏrŏ ch'ingsonghanŭn uri suryŏngnim* [*Worldwide Support for Kim Il Sung*] (Pyongyang: Chosŏn girok kwahak yŏnghwa ch'waryŏngso, 2012). In this article, both versions are referenced.

18.
Kang Su-myŏng, *Segye-rŭl anŭshigo* [*Hugging the World*] (Pyongyang: Kŭmsŏng ch'ŏngnyŏn ch'ulp'ansa, 2012), 64.
19.
Paek, 396–397.

20.
"Kukchejŏk yŏpcho-ŭi pinnanŭn mobŏm-ŭl ch'angjohashin pulmyŏl-ŭi ŏpchŏk" [Immortal Achievement in Creating a Shining Example of International Cooperation], *Rodong Sinmun*, January 31, 2019.

to the newly independent countries. Such support was an expression of Kim's international leadership. At the same time, the film ends with a tour of the International Friendship Exhibition in Myohyangsan (Mt. Myohyang), where gifts received from around the world by Kim Il Sung are displayed. Leaders from the world's five continents and people of various ranks and titles gave 166,000 gifts as a sign of gratitude to Kim, who was "a shining leader who achieved brilliant achievements before history and humanity." This International Friendship Exhibition is a space showing "the world in North Korea."[21] However, the world of the International Friendship Exhibition is also a "suspended world" after the deaths of Kim Il Sung and Kim Jong Il. In the 2010s, North Korea could not do anything but display the North Korea of the 1980s, when it strove to globalize its Juche ideology.

As Kim Jong Un came to power in 2011, North Korea commemorated the unconditional aid, international cooperation, and loyalty of the Kim Il Sung era.[22] The overseas activities of Mansudae Overseas Project Group's creative history, as tracked by Che Onejoon, can also be interpreted as the restoration of the North Korean globalization effort in the 1980s. *Far Away from My Fatherland*, a novel based on a true story, shares the same atmosphere and flow of time. Che's documentary project is a valuable resource that offers new interpretations.

Our Great Leader who received the greatest glory of the people

Fig. 1
Worldwide Support for Kim Il Sung, 2017, HD video, 7min 46sec

21.
For the meaning of the International Friendship Exhibition, see Heonik Kwon and Byung-ho Chung, *North Korea: Beyond Charismatic Politics* (Paju: Changbi, 2013), 190–197.

22.
Jiyoung Kim, "Understanding North Korea's Perspective on Foreign Aid: A Content Analysis of Rodong Newspaper," *International Development and Cooperation Review* 11, no. 3. (Seoul: Korea Association International Development and Cooperation, 2019) 34–35.

The Gifts from Africa

Monumental Tour

Che Onejoon

The fanatical image of Pyongyang citizens mourning in front of the statue of Kim Il Sung at his funeral in 1994 came as a shock to many people. Perhaps being driven by such a memory, whenever considering North Korean arts, what comes to mind first is the statue of Kim Il Sung. North Korean art is externally referred to as socialist realist art and internally as Juche (self-reliance) art. However, I would consider North Korean art as part of the history of surrealism, because it seems to project an excessive heroism that goes beyond realism and sometimes portrays what looks like a fantasy world.

When I first heard the news that North Korea had built a monument in Africa, I mistakenly assumed that the North had built a monument to their Juche propaganda in Africa. North Korea was unfamiliar, but the combination of Africa and the North was even more unfamiliar. On the other hand, however, being able to see North Korean monuments in Africa meant that I could glimpse North Korea through Africa. As an artist, I wanted to re-examine North Korea's art and architecture in terms of aesthetics and history and in relation to Africa, rather than looking at the country through the tragic prism of fratricidal war or an ideological confrontation. My project started in 2012[1] and has continued until the present, presenting historical, political, and cultural perspectives on the issue through the forms of photography, film, and installation. In this article, I will give a brief overview of the direction of North Korea's diplomacy in Africa and examine the cases of Senegal, Namibia, and Zimbabwe, which raised controversies around the world with regards to statues, monuments, and buildings built by North Koreans.

Mansudae Overseas Projects

Mansudae Overseas Projects is a subsidiary of North Korea's Mansudae Art Studio. It is known to have built statues, monuments, and architecture in eighteen African countries—Senegal, Gabon, Burkina Faso, Togo, Benin, Congo, Democratic Republic of the Congo, Tanzania, Angola, Namibia, Botswana, Zimbabwe, Mozambique, Madagascar, Ethiopia, Sudan, Central African Republic, and Chad—from the late 1970s until recently.

North Korea's construction diplomacy / business in Africa can be divided into two different periods. The first is the 1980s when the country built sculptures and structures for African countries without charging money. The North Korean sculptures and buildings from this period can be regarded as the result of the diplomatic competition between the two Koreas in Africa.[2] After the Korean War, issues around the Korean peninsula, such as the fragile peace, the ceasefire line, and the presence of US troops became annual agenda items of the United Nations, which were decided through the voting of member states.[3] In the late 1960s, many newly independent African countries joined the UN. Then, Kim Il Sung, the Supreme Leader of North Korea at the time, launched construction diplomacy in Africa to gain support from the new African countries. Starting with the gratis construction of a monument to the 10th anniversary of the establishment of the communist government in Ethiopia in 1982, North Korea went on to build the National Assembly of the Central African Republic, a statue of president Bongo in Gabon, and the presidential residence in Madagascar, all free of charge. The buildings and monuments in Africa, along with the Children & Youth Palace in Sudan, appear in a documentary film from the period, which was produced to show off the greatness of Kim Il Sung. What is interesting in this film is the Africans who praise Kim. In fact, many of the people I met in different countries in Africa showed their gratitude to North Korea, considering the buildings constructed free of charge by North Koreans to be the result of the friendship between leaders.

After the "Arduous March" famine of the mid 1990s that coincided with the rapid economic deterioration of North Korea, Kim Jong Il took charge of the country's diplomacy. From that moment, the country stopped its gratis construction in Africa and began receiving orders to build monuments and construct buildings in exchange for compensation. The African Renaissance Monument, completed in Senegal in 2010, served as an occasion for Mansudae Overseas Projects to become widely known internationally through the international media.

1.
International Friendship (2017–2018) is a multimedia installation consisting of three-channel video documentary *Mansudae Master Class*, photographs, sculptures, and archives.

2.
Gabon is the place where the South-North competition for the establishment of diplomatic relations with the Third World countries is most evident through architecture. North Korea maintained close ties with then-president Omar Bongo, building two statues in his hometown Franceville in the 1980s (free of charge) and in the 2000s (in exchange for compensation). During the Park Chung-hee regime, the South Korean govern-ment also signed a medical cooperation agreement with Gabon and further established economic, technological, cultural, and scientific agreements with the country, strengthening diplomatic ties and treating its president as a state guest when he visited South Korea. During the period, the South Korean government spent a large sum of money to build a high-end department store Renovation (Yusin Department Store), fifteen stories tall and covering 14,000-square meters in Gabon. The government also sent South Korean employees to work in that building.

3.
The Geneva Conference in April 1954, held according to the UN General Assembly Resolution 711(VII) with sixteen participating countries along with North

Senegal

In May 2010, the news that Mansudae Overseas Projects has built a 49-meter high African Renaissance Monument in Dakar, Senegal's capital, was reported around the world. Many people were surprised to know that North Korean artists built the tallest monument in Africa with their advanced technique of statue making, which they had accumulated by creating statues of Kim Il Sung and Kim Jong Il.[4]

The African Renaissance Monument, which depicts a couple holding a child pointing somewhere, was conceived by president Abdoulaye Wade, the third president of Senegal. It is said that Wade had a dream in which he saw a young African couple climbing a mountain with their child. He then called Senegalese architect Pierre Goudiaby Atepa to commission the project. In 2009, even before the monument was completed, there was a large protest against the construction of the monument. When the media uncovered the fact that the government had paid a total of 27 million dollars to North Korea for the statue, a protest took place in the capital, Dakar, calling for a scrapping of the construction of such a large monument. There were violent clashes between protesters and police throughout the city. The reasons for the objection were: first, the construction budget of 27 million dollars was enough to solve the unemployment in Senegal to some extent; second, the budget should prioritize the construction of sewer systems in the city. However, the biggest problem was raised by the religious community, which was that the large-scale monument was opposed to Muslim teachings. In addition, the Muslim Imams claimed that it was unacceptable because the female figure of the statue exposed more than half of her breasts, which was against the image of a Muslim country that strictly restricted the exposure of women's bodies. They insisted that such was unacceptable in a country where more than 90% of the population was Muslim. When I visited the monument for the third time in 2015, it had already become a tourist attraction, with a number of visitors that was more than enough to forget the negative public opinions at home and abroad. The illuminated bronze glows a golden hue and stands out when seen from Dakar's airport. From an aesthetic point of view, a formatively unfamiliar shape often looks very strange depending on the viewing angle, and such an intense shape is often interpreted as a result of Stalinist machismo.

Namibia

If the African Renaissance Monument in Senegal was an opportunity to introduce the North Korea skill at large-scale sculptures and bronze casting to the world, what happened in Namibia presented North Korea's architectural style, which gained more attention as the UN's economic sanctions against North Korea began. Due to North Korea's sixth nuclear test in September 2017, a clause to put a ban on UN member states from "providing work authorizations for DPRK nationals" was added to the UN Security Council Resolution No. 2375. Namibia had been a long-time ally of North Korea, even violating UN sanctions against North Korea. In particular, Namibia's first president Sam Nujoma was very close to Kim Il Sung.[5] Sam Nujoma served as president from 1990, when Namibia gained independence, to 2005. He granted the North Korean government a monopoly on construction of government buildings in the country. Such a monopolistic attitude of the North Korean government received a lot of criticism from the locals. John Grobler, an investigative journalist in Namibia, has brought the issue to the international spotlight and written several critical articles, arguing for example:

> Just why the North Koreans have a headlock over all contracts to build national monuments in Namibia on a no-bid basis remains a mystery. Their workmanship is poor and Heroes' Acre, completed in 2002 for about R100-million, is already falling apart and undergoing renovations. There are some obvious clues: The eight-meter statue of The Unknown Soldier towering over Heroes' Acre is very clearly that of Namibia's founding president Sam Nujoma. Like the Kims of North Korea, Nujoma venerates the mythology of military struggle, even though neither he nor the Kims ever saw much military action. It is hazy what exactly the real nature of Namibia's official relationship with the North Koreans is. But what is clear is that North Korea enjoys something of a special relationship with Namibia's ageing leadership: each of these prestige ventures has been a pet project

Korea, the People's Republic of China, and the Soviet Union, ran from April 26 until June 15. However, the political conference on the unification of Korea broke down and the Korean issues were discussed again at the United Nations assembly. At that time, the United Nations General Assembly automatically included the annual report of the UN Commission on the Reunification of Korea (UNCURK) in the agenda of the next General Assembly, which led to the annual discu-ssion of the Korean issue ever since.

The main issue of the confrontation was support for the resolution by Western countries, which focused on the general election in both North and South Korea under the supervision of the United Nations, as well as support from the communist bloc and non-aligned countries for the withdrawal of US forces, the dissolution of the UN Korean Commission (its mission ended in 1973), and the dissolution of the UN Command on the peninsula. In most cases, the West's proposal to maintain the UN's principles

of inter-Korean unification and UNCURK were adopted by an overwhelming majority. However, the resolutions of both sides were introduced almost automatically every year, and the UN General Assembly Hall became a place for tedious exchanges of annual political attacks on the Korean issue (Source: National Archives of Korea).

4.
It is known that there have been more than 70 large statues and 30,000 plaster busts of Kim Il

The Gifts from Africa

of Nujoma, and awarded to Mansudae without any tender. The projects include renovations to Nujoma's private home on his Etunda farm, according to documents seen by the *Mail & Guardian*.[6]

Standing approximately ten kilometers away from Namibia's capital, Windhoek, is the Heroes' Acre. It is a national memorial facility that opened in August 2002. It is told that the Heroes' Acre was commissioned to Mansudae Overseas Projects after president Nujoma's visit to Pyongyang. Commissioned with a request to resemble Taesongsan Revolutionary Martyrs' Cemetery, it can be said that the Heroes' Acre is actually close to being a replica of the North Korean cemetery. Similar to Taesongsan Revolutionary Martyrs' Cemetery, the Heroes' Acre is tiered on the hillside in the form of a park with seats that can accommodate 5,000 people. At the top of the hill, there is an eight-meter high statue to commemorate unknown soldiers. A total of 174 independence heroes are enshrined in the Heroes' Acre, and it is also known that graves for surviving freedom fighters have already been established. It is interesting that the statue of the Unknown Soldier has a face quite similar to that of Nujoma when he was younger. Therefore, the statue is full of Nujoma's yearning to mythicize himself. In addition to the Heroes' Acre, Mansudae Overseas Projects also constructed the Presidential Palace, Independence Memorial Museum, and Military Museum. It also built other unknown buildings to different scales, which also include private company buildings.

The Independence Memorial Museum is built with an intense golden façade as if the building was covered in gold. The edge of the building is decorated with black marble to emphasize the stronger vertical frontality. The vertical composition and symmetry, which are characteristic of North Korean buildings, are shown in contrast to the monotonous buildings around the museum. They come a more overwhelming image. When I visited the museum for the second time after it opened its doors to the public in April 2014, I could see the exhibits. All interior decorations and paintings, except for trophies from the civil war and memorabilia from veterans, were produced in Pyongyang by North Korean artists at Mansudae Art Studio and transported to Namibia. Some large murals were produced on site as

well. There was a note to record the number of visitors at the entrance of the museum. Although there was no admission fee to enter the museum, approximately twenty to thirty people visited the museum on weekdays. Considering the population of Windhoek (325,858 people), there were not that many visitors. Nevertheless, the Independence Memorial Museum was located in the center of the city, and it seemed to be a representative building of the country and a kind of landmark.

Zimbabwe

In Zimbabwe, North Korea stands on a dark page of the country's modern history. Similar to Namibia's Sam Nujoma, Zimbabwe's former president Robert Gabriel Mugabe, the country's former president and the world's longest-serving dictator, began to build close relations with North Korea in the 1970s when Kim Il Sung reinforced diplomatic efforts for Africa. Mugabe was so deeply moved by Kim Il Sung's Juche ideology that he even put a complete English translation of Juche ideology in Zimbabwe's major government offices. In 1981, a year after Zimbabwe officially gained independence from Britain, Mansudae Overseas Projects built the National Heroes' Acre outside Harare.

The National Heroes' Acre is a place to accommodate the bodies of soldiers who died in the Rhodesian Bush War (1966–1979),[7] which was a clash between the Zimbabwe African National Union (ZANU) under Mugabe's command and the Zimbabwe African People's Union (ZAPU) under the command of the former vice-president Joshua Nkomo. In this sense, it can be said that it is a place that commemorates the most important event in Zimbabwe's modern history. The National Heroes' Acre is located along Harare-Bulawayo road, approximately seven kilometers away from Harare, the country's capital. The geographical conditions are very similar to the Heroes' Acre in Namibia. Although both the facilities are known to be a bit far from the capital, visitors feel quite a lot of distance since they are surrounded by an endless array of wasteland and roads. The National Heroes' Acre is said to be produced by seven artists from North Korea's Mansudae Art Studio and ten Zimbabwean artists. At first glance, a statue with a composition that is similar to that of Juche Tower in Pyongyang comes into view, with strikingly realistic details that follow

Sung erected throughout North Korea. There is a lot of information on the Internet that there are more than 30,000 statues of Kim Il Sung alone. However, according to North Korean defectors, the number includes plaster figures as well.
5.
Namibia was under the colonial rule of Germany until the early 20th century and called "German South West Africa." After 1915, the country was colonized again by South Africa for 74 years. In March

1990, it became the 53rd country in Africa to gain independence. Between 1966 and 1990, the country was engaged in a war of independence with South Africa. It was a guerrilla war led by SWAPO (South-West Africa People's Organization) under Nujoma's command. During the independence movement, Namibia received support from pro-Soviet countries. In particular, North Korea is known to have provided a lot of military support. North Korea offered free supplies, including weapons,

to PLAN (People's Liberation Army of Namibia), which was an armed wing of SWAPO. From 1965, many SWAPO party members received training in Pyongyang.
6.
John Grobler, "North Korea's deals in Namibia a mystery," *Mail & Guardian*, April 26, 2013.
7.
The invasion turned Zimbabwe into a British colony called Southern Rhodesia and formally

the socialist realism that is unique to North Korean art. Thanks to such a first impression, one might feel as if he was brought to a memorial facility in Pyongyang, North Korea. This peculiarity gives a sense of unfamiliarity that does not match the surrounding environment, which is similar to the Heroes' Acre in Namibia.

In 2010, North Korea erected a statue of former vice-president Joshua Nkomo in Bulawayo, the former capital of Zimbabwe. On the inauguration day of the statue, Nkomo's bereaved family and local residents forced the statue to be removed since they thought it was insulting to have North Korea produce it. With the international media coverage, the incident became an international controversy. North Korea's involvement in Mugabe regime's Gukurahundi massacre also contributed to the removal of the statue, which in turn raised the media attention to the incident.[8] In 1983, North Korea dispatched 130 military instructors and advisors upon Mugabe's request, training the Fifth Brigade, which was a dedicated unit to protect Mugabe. In Bulawayo region, North Korea has become as unwelcome as Mugabe, the perpetrator of the massacre.

The torn-down statue of Nkomo is deserted in the backyard of the Natural Museum of Zimbabwe, wrapped in a tarpaulin. Contrary to what I had expected, the statue resembled Nkomo and appeared to shine with a classy, brassy yellow gleam. I found some critical news articles on the statue saying that it had a disproportionally small face, but I came to think that it might have been a simple misconception by the local residents as they looked up the statue from the ground. Similar to statues in other African countries that had been made by artists from Mansudae Art Studio, the Nkomo statue showed realistic depiction and the advanced technique of the North Korean sculptors.

North Korean Art
In addition to the examples of the three countries mentioned so far, Mansudae Art Studio has built a number of monuments and statues in many African countries. However, the discussion about North Korea usually focuses on its political relationship with African countries, the opaque bidding process, and the suspicion that North Korea's business to earn foreign currency is linked to the accumulation of the country's slush fund. As in the case of the three countries, the interpretation of North Korean architecture and art in Africa is influenced by political opinions. As such, they are interpreted only as objects of political happenings without any involvement of art criticism. Therefore, there is a lack of understanding and criticism on the aesthetics of North Korean buildings and statues, even in the very countries where such creations exist.

North Korea's architecture and art absorbed socialist realism and Russian neoclassicism in their early stage of development. Since 1967, however, nationalism was introduced to socialist content, internalizing the Juche ideology.[9] The buildings, statues, and monuments in African countries mentioned in the earlier part of this article materialize the architectural theory based on North Korea's Juche ideology of creating architecture for the people, emphasizing the socialist realism style while not forsaking practicality by employing horizontal and vertical structures, a sense of large volume, and emphasis on heroic images (idolization). With the demise of the Eastern bloc under communism in 1989, socialist art disappeared around the world. However, North Korea kept developing its socialist realist art by adding a nationalist style as a propaganda tool for the Juche idea, ultimately exporting it to African countries.

The building and statues built by North Korea in Africa are expected to show a mixture of North Korean socialist realist style and regional indigenousness of African art. However, the Heroes' Acre in Namibia shows a similar design with Taesongsan Revolutionary Martyrs' Cemetery and the National Heroes' Acre in Zimbabwe shows a resemblance to the statue at the Juche Tower in Pyongyang. These examples show that Mansudae Overseas Projects did not consider the sentiment of the locals, pushing forward the characteristics of socialist realist art into African countries.

It is now necessary to think about what the African leaders were trying to achieve by bringing North Korean art and architecture into their countries. As mentioned earlier, North Korea laid the foundation for Juche architecture through the debate over nationalist forms in the 1960s and completed the idea of Juche architecture in the 1970s and 1980s. In his preface to *On The Art of Architecture*, Kim Jong Il wrote, "In the course of creating the architecture of our own style through the architect-

incorporated it into British territory in 1923. With the independence of African colonies in the 1960s, the British colonial policy changed, allowing independence as a condition of creating a system in which black citizens could represent themselves. However, in 1964, the Rhodesian Front, led by Ian Douglas Smith, resolutely rejected the British government's policy of "no independence before majority rule" and maintained white domination, declaring unilateral independence in 1963. The Rhodesia Bush War was a guerrilla war started by black citizens who protested against this white supremacist regime.

8.
The Gukurahundi was a series of massacres of Ndebele civilians carried out by the Zimbabwe National Army from early 1983 to late 1987. It derives from a Shona language term which loosely translates to "the early rain which washes away the chaff before the spring rains."

The Gukurahundi massacres remain the darkest period in the country's post-independence history, when more than 20,000 civilians were killed by Robert Mugabe's feared Fifth Brigade. "New documents claim to prove Mugabe ordered Gukurahundi killings," *The Guardian*, May 19, 2015. https://www.theguardian.com/world/2015/may/19/mugabe-zimbabwe-gukurahundi-massacre-matabeleland.

The Gifts from Africa

ural revolution, the Juche theory of architecture has been systematized, the relationships between architecture and society, and between architecture and man have been clarified fully on an absolutely scientific basis, and the theory of architectural creation, the theory of architectural formation and the method of guidance that must be consistently maintained by the party of the working class have been established." On the surface, architecture with scientific qualities, legitimacy, revolutionary nature, and originality based on the demands of the people can be seen as the gist of Juche architecture. However, it played a role in emphasizing the absoluteness of the leader since the 1970s, as the authority of its execution fell under the hands of Kim Il Sung and Kim Jong Il. It is assumed that the African leaders wanted to transplant North Korea's theory of art and architecture into their own countries.

At this point, it is necessary to recall the fact that the gratuitous buildings and statues built by the Kim Il Sung regime were maintained over three decades despite the fact that they were built without any consideration of local sentiment, becoming historical buildings and monuments in different African countries. The heterogeneous contrast that those buildings and statues generate with their surroundings no longer remains as a bizarre sight but becomes an impressive spectacle, which invites us to reflect on the power of North Korean art and architecture. Even if the symbolism of North Korean buildings and statues in Africa signifies a dictatorial regime, nuclear weapons, and the outdated socialist realist aesthetics, we cannot simply consider it as a basis to ignore the authentic aesthetic value of North Korean art in African countries.

North Korean statues, monuments, and buildings in African countries would not exist without the division of the Korean peninsula. Thus, these statues, monuments, and buildings are evidence of the division of North and South Korea and the global Cold War history. As examined in this article, they function as important indicators to understand the culture and arts, international politics and diplomacy, and economy of the two Koreas and African countries. North Korean art in African countries is of great significance to us as it allows us to interpret the history of diplomacy between North Korea and African countries, which has not been known well to us,

from a different view. Thus, I wanted to break free from a kind of Orientalism towards North Korea, caused by misunderstanding and ignorance of the country. In my archive work, I put effort into arranging diverse historical materials and images across a number of different dimensions. In my video practice, I conducted many interviews to present different opinions and produced a three-channel documentary film with a structure that crosses the three regions of South Korea, North Korea, and Africa. Through this project, I hope to invite viewers to reflect on the relationship between Africa and the Korean peninsula in Korea's history of art and diplomacy across the various dimensions of politics, history, and aesthetics.

9.
In the 1960s, North Korea laid the groundwork for Juche architecture through the debate over nationalist forms. The idea of Juche architecture was established through the 1970s and 1980s. During that period, Kim Jong Il expressed the achievements of his father Kim Kim Il Sung through architecture and art. He displayed his leadership as a successor and leader by developing architecture as a mass mobilization project. In 1992, he compiled his views on art and architecture in a publication *On The Art of Architecture*.

List of Works

P. 5
*Bust of Former President
Laurent Kabila,
sculpted in 2002*
Kinshasa, DR Congo, 2013
Digital C-print, 60×75cm

P. 6–7
*Statue of DR Congo's
first Prime Minister
Patrice Lumumba, sculpted in 2002*
Kinshasa, DR Congo, 2013
Digital C-print, 60×78cm

P. 8
Ave du Cercle. Kinshasa
DR Congo, 2013
Digital C-print, 60×88cm

P. 10–11
Pumping Stations, built in the 1970s
Madagascar, 2015
Digital C-print 60×86cm

P. 12
*North Korea Laborers' Dormitory #1,
built in the 1970s*
Madagascar, 2015
Digital C-print, 60×86cm

P. 13
*North Korea Laborers' Dormitory #2,
built in the 1970s*
Madagascar, 2015
Digital C-print, 60×86cm

P. 14–15
Iavoloha Palace, built in the 1970s
Antananarivo, Madagascar, 2015
Digital C-print, 60×86cm

P. 16
New Chinese Company
Windhoek, Namibia, 2013
Digital C-print, 60×77cm

P. 17
Freemasons Hall
Robert Mugabe Avenue,
Windhoek, Namibia, 2013
Digital C-print, 60×77cm

P. 18–19
*Military Museum, built in 2004
but still not open to the public*
Okahandja, Namibia, 2015
Digital C-print, 60×86cm

P. 20–21
Hero's Acre, built in 2002
Windhoek, Namibia, 2013
Digital C-print, 60×86cm

P. 22
*Interior of the Independence
Memorial Museum #2*
Windhoek, Namibia, 2015
Digital C-print, 60×84cm

P. 23
*Interior of the Independence
Memorial Museum #1*
Windhoek, Namibia, 2015
Digital C-print, 60×84cm

P. 24
*Glory to the Heroes,
Independence Memorial Museum*
Windhoek, Namibia, 2015
Digital C-print, 60×75cm

P. 25
*Long Live Namibian Independence,
Independence Memorial Museum*
Windhoek, Namibia, 2015
Digital C-print, 60×75cm

P. 26–27
*Statue of Former President Sam Nujoma,
Independence Memorial Museum*
Windhoek, Namibia, 2015
Digital C-print, 60×84cm

P. 28–29
*Independence Memorial Museum
under Construction*
Windhoek, Namibia, 2013
Digital C-print, 60×88cm

P. 31
*Statue of Sam Nujoma,
Independence Memorial Museum*
Windhoek, Namibia, 2016
Digital C-print, 60×86cm

P. 32
Mugabe Street
Windhoek, Namibia, 2013
Digital C-print, 60×86cm

P. 33
Darth Vader SWAPO
Windhoek, Namibia, 2013
Digital C-print, 60×84cm

P. 35
*ZANU-PF (Zimbabwe African
National Union–Patriotic Front)
Campaign Office*
Bulawayo, Zimbabwe, 2013
Digital C-print, 60×86cm

P. 36
8th Avenue
Bulawayo, Zimbabwe, 2015
Digital C-print, 60×86cm

P. 37
*Statue of Former Vice-President Joshua Nkomo,
rebuilt by Zimbabwean Artist in 2014*
Bulawayo, Zimbabwe, 2015
Digital C-print, 60×86cm

Rodong Sinmun (Official Newspaper of the Central Committee of the Workers' Party of Korea), P. 102, 103

P. 102

"We demand the dismantlement of the United Nations Command and the removal of all troops from South Korea: Botswana Representative."
November 1, 1975.

"The Great Leader Comrade Kim Il Sung sent a congratulatory message to the President of the Republic of Zaire Mobutu Sese Seko."
November 22, 1975.

"The United Nations Command must be disbanded and every foreign armed force must be withdrawn from South Korea. President of Mali Moussa Traoré's Speech at the UN General Assembly."
December 1, 1975.

"To the Chairman of the Liberation Front of Mozambique Samora Machel. Kim Il Sung, General Secretary of the Workers' Party of Korea."
September 25, 1974.

"(Above) "The unification of Korea should be achieved in peace without the interference of others. President of Rwanda Juvénal Habyarimana's Speech at the UN General Assembly."
(Middle) "We urge that the foreign militaries in South Korea should withdraw from the country. President of Republic of Equatorial Guinea Teodoro Obiang Nguema Mbasogo's Speech at the UN General Assembly."
(Below) "The biggest obstacle to the unification of Korea is the interference by America in internal affairs. President of Libya Muammar Gaddafi's Speech at the UN General Assembly."
October 29, 1975.

P. 103

"Groundbreaking ceremony for cement plant in Somalia." Year unknown.

(Above) "UN General Assembly to discuss the Korea issue. The joint resolutions of more than 40 countries suggest realistic and rational solutions to the Korea problem. Speech by the Delegation from Tanzania."
(Below) "The United Nations should help the unification of Korea. Speech by the Senegalese Representative."
October 30, 1975.

"The government of Togo breaks off diplomatic relations with South Korean puppet government, the President of Togo calls an emergency meeting of the Central Committee of the Rally of the Togolese People."
September 19, 1974.

(Above) "I support people's stance in the DPRK demanding the withdrawal of foreign armed forces from South Korea, emphasized by the President of Uganda."
(Below) "Korea cannot be divided in two, it is always to be one, emphasized by the President of the Republic of Equatorial Guinea."
May 21, 1973.

"The people of the Republic of Zaire acknowledge that the unification of Korea is an issue for the people of Korea to deal with without interference by other parties. President of the Republic of Zaire Zaire, Edouard Mokolo Wa Mpombo's Speech at the UN General Assembly."
October 4, 1973.

P. 104, 105

Pages from a Catalogue of the *Mansudae Overseas Project Group of Companies*

P. 104

(Above)
Former President of Angola
Agostinho Neto
Former President of Togo
Gnassingbé Eyadéma
Former President of
DR Congo
Marien Ngouabi

(Below)
Former President of
Mozambique
Samora Machel
Former President of Gabon
Omar Bongo
Former President of Egypt
Hosni Mubarak

P. 105

(Above)
People's Artist
Architectural Drafter
Kim Yŏng-sŏp
Meritorious Artist
Sculptor
U Ŭng-ho
Meritorious Artist
Architectural Drafter
Jŏng Kyŏng-pal

(Middle)
Kim Il Sung Laurel Wreath Winner
People's Artist
Sculptor
Ryu Ha-yŏl
People's Artist
Sculptor
Kim Sŭng-si
People's Artist
Statue Artist
Paek Man-gil

(Below)
Kim Il Sung Laurel Wreath Winner
Hero of Labor
People's Artist
Sculptor
O Dae-hyŏng
People's Artist
Sculptor
Ri Pyŏng-il
Kim Il Sung Laurel Wreath Winner
Hero of Labor
People's Artist
Sculptor
Ro Ik-hwa

P. 106, 107

African Renaissance Monument under Construction, 2008–2009. Photo Courtesy of ATEPA Group

P. 108

Daily Production Report, June 21, 2010–February 3, 2011. The third group comprises eighteen North Korean workers. Found discarded in Namibia in February 2013.

Monday, June 21
4 out of 18 working, crane
Tuesday, June 22
4 out of 18 working, crane

(Left)
Construction site of Independence Museum
Total land area 4,000m²
Building area 1,143m²
1st floor 836m²
2nd floor 836m²
28.5 599m²
34.5 836m²
39 716m²
Circumference of column 14.55m
Two corridors on each side of the 12th floor, stairs on the 1st floor

Friday, November 12, 2010
13 of 18 workers
Food, Warehouse, Machinery, Expenses and Housework
Group B
Jung-sik, Tong-sik, Thae-hŭng
Group A
Jun-sam, Yŏng-min, Kwang-sŏng, Yŏng-jŏng 120+300
Group C
Sang-won, Tong-hyŏk, Jong-nam 120+300

(Right)
Saturday, November 13, 2010
14 of 18 workers
Food, Warehouse, Machinery, Expenses
Group B
Nam-hyŏk, Tong-sik 23.2m²
Group A
Jun-sam, Yŏng-min, Kwang-sung 23.2m²
Group C
Sang-won, Tong-hyŏk, Jong-nam 120+300

Sunday, November 14, 2010
14 of 18 workers
Food, Warehouse, Machinery, Expenses
Group B
Nam-hyŏk , Jung-sik, Tong-sik, Thae-hŭng
Group A
Jun-sam, Yŏng-min, Kwang-sŏng, Yŏng-jŏng
Group C
Sang-won, Sŭng-hyŏk, Jong-nam, Jun-myŏng
Total 8 Hours

(Left)
Weight of walls
3000×1 = 112kg
1500×1 = 56kg
2400×1 = 93kg

(Right)
Water 3l, Cement, Sand
One stair 0.2m²
One stair 0.4m²

(Above)
Tuesday, January 4, 2011
12 of 17 workers

(Below)
Sunday, January 9, 2011
13 of 17 workers

P. 109

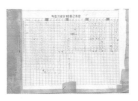

Attendance Sheet for North Korean Workers at Independence Museum in September, Year unknown. Found discarded in Namibia in February 2013.

Attendance Sheet for North Korean Workers at Independence Museum in July 2010. Found discarded in Namibia in February 2013.

Worker's names, in order they are listed:
Son Yong-sŏk, Kim Hŭi-bok, Kim Nam-chŏl, Kim Kwang-myŏng, Song Sang-won, Kim Yŏng-il, Choe Jong-sik, Ko Kyŏng-sŏng, Kim Jun-myŏng, Park Hyŏ-chŏl, Kim Tong-sik, Cha Tae-hong, Kim Yong-chŏl, Kim Jun-sam, Ri Il-sang, Ri Sŭng-hyŏk, Kim Yŏngmin, Park Chŏl-nam

Blueprint of Independence Museum, Made by Mansudae Overseas Project Group of Companies, Windhoek, Namibia. Found discarded in Namibia in February 2013.

P. 110

Tourists in front of Statue of Former Vice-President Joshua Nkomo, Bulawayo, Zimbabwe, 2015. Photo by a souvenir photographer

P. 111

Tourists in front of African Renaissance Monument, Dakar, Senegal, 2015. Photo by a souvenir photographer

P. 112

Poster of Hero's Acre, Ticket Office of Hero's Acre, 2015, Harare, Zimbabwe, Dimensions variable

P. 129
Solidarity (wood sculpture)
from Apollo Milton Opeto Obote,
President of the Republic of Uganda
and Chairman of Uganda People's Congress
[December Juche70 (1981)], 2017
Dimensions variable

P. 130
Solidarity (wood sculpture)
from Samora Moisés Machel,
President of People's Republic of Mozambique
[September Juche72 (1983)], 2017
Dimensions variable

P. 131
Solidarity (wood sculpture)
from National Democratic Party Ghana
[July Juche82 (1993)], 2017
Dimensions variable

P. 132
Saharan Gypsum Desert Rose
from People's Democratic Republic of Algeria
[February Juche71 (1982)], 2017
Dimensions variable

P. 133
Tree Model
from Samora Moisés Machel,
President of People's Republic of Mozambique
[September Juche72 (1983)], 2017
Dimensions variable

P. 134
Clock Box
from Muammar Al Gaddafi,
Brotherly Leader of the Great Socialist
People's Libyan Arab Jamahiriya
[December Juche70 (1981)], 2017
Dimensions variable

P. 135
Wall Clock
from the Committee of Great Juche Idea Study
of the United Nations Institute for Namibia in Zambia
[December Juche73 (1984)], 2017
 Dimensions variable

P. 136
Carved Ivory and Chief of Bantu Tribe (bronze sculpture)
 from Mobutu Sese Seko Kuku Ngbendu Wa Za Banga,
President of the Republic of Zaire
[September Juche77 (1988)], 2017
Dimensions variable

P. 137
Ivory
from Gnassingbé Eyadéma,
President of Togolese Republic
[September Juche70 (1981)], 2017
Dimensions variable

P. 138
Crane (horn craft)
from Siaka Probyn Stevens,
President of the Republic of Sierra Leone
[April Juche71 (1982)], 2017
Dimensions variable

P. 139
Wall Clock
from St. Andrews Kingston Juche Study of Jamaica
[February Juche72 (1983)], 2017
Dimensions variable

P. 140
(Above)
Crocodile (ivory carving)
Butterfly Specimen from Ahmed Sékou Touré,
President of the People's Revolutionary
Republic of Guinea
[November Juche72 (1983)], 2017
Dimensions variable
(Below)
Elephant (wood sculpture)
from Department of Political Science,
Somali National University
[July Juche72 (1983)], 2017
Dimensions variable

P. 141
(Above)
Natural Crystal, Crystal Orb
from Didier Ratsiraka,
President of the Democratic Republic
of Madagascar
[October Juche79 (1990)], 2017
Dimensions variable
(Below)
Friendly Bridge (ivory craft)
from the College of Music and Drama,
Khartoum, Democratic Republic of Sudan
[February Juche73 (1984)], 2017
Dimensions variable

P. 142
(Above)
Copper Tray
Standing Secretary of the Ministry
of Sports and Culture of Zimbabwe
[July Juche75 (1986)], 2017
Dimensions variable
(Below)
Pencil Vase
Juche Study Group of Guyana
[February Juche70 (1981)], 2017
Dimensions variable

P. 143
(Above)
Wall Decoration
from Mathieu Kérékou,
President of the People's Republic of Benin
[September Juche72 (1983)], 2017
Dimensions variable
(Below)
Procession of the King of Abomey (bronze sculpture)
from Mathieu Kérékou,
President of the People's Republic of Benin
[September Juche69 (1970)], 2017
Dimensions variable

P. 144
Peasant and Artist of Madagascar (wood sculpture)
from Prime Minister of the Republic of Madagascar
[September Juche72 (1983)], 2017
Dimensions variable

The Gifts from Africa

P. 145
Hunter
from Sudanese Socialist Union
[October Juche73 (1984)], 2017
Dimensions variable

P. 146
Electric Clock (ivory craft)
from Robert Mugabe,
Prime Minister of the Republic of Zimbabwe
[July Juche72 (1983)], 2017
Dimensions variable

P. 147
(Above)
Bronze Carved Elephant
From Canaan Banana,
President of Zimbabwe
[September Juche72 (1983)], 2017
Dimensions variable
(Below)
Bronze Carved Elephant
Delegation to the Republic
of Zimbabwen Labor Union
[August Juche72 (1983)], 2017
Dimensions variable

P. 148
(Left)
Electric Table Clock
from Nigerian Military Delegate
[June Juche83 (1994)], 2017
Dimensions variable
(Right)
Patriarch's Chair, Cloth, Hat, Necklace, Armrest and Baton
from J.O Mama,
Chief of Umuoji Tribe
Federal Republic of Nigeria
[April Juche84 (1994)], 2017
Dimensions variable

P. 149
(Left)
Antelope, Mortar, and Knife (wood sculpture)
from Permanent Secretary of Socialist Party of Senegal
[February Juche71 (1982)], 2017
Dimensions variable
(Right)
Brass Teapot, Brass Plate, and Drinking Glass
from the Association of African Journalists and Writers
[July Juche72 (1983)], 2017
Dimensions variable

P. 150
(Left)
Bronze Sculpture
from Committees for the Defense
of the Revolution of Burkina Faso
[September Juche74 (1985)], 2017
Dimensions variable
(Right)
Warrior (wood sculpture)
from Enugu State Government of Nigeria
[April Juche84 (1995)], 2017
Dimensions variable

P. 151
(Left)
Cavalryman (bronze sculpture)
from Paul Biya,
President of Republic of Cameroon
[November Juche73 (1984)], 2017
Dimensions variable
(Right)
Musician (wood sculpture)
from Joseph Saidu Momoh,
President of Republic of Sierra Leone
[April Juche81 (1992)], 2017
Dimensions variable

P. 152
Solidarity (ivory carving)
from the National Coordination Committee of Juche Study
Dar es Salaam University College of Education
[February Juche71 (1982)], 2017
Dimensions variable

P. 153
Busan Biennale 2018,
Divided We Stand
curated by Cristina Ricupero and Jörg Heiser.
Museum of Contemporary Art Busan, S. Korea

P. 154–155
Kuandu Biennale 2018,
Seven Questions for Asia, Freedom, What Was That All About?
curated by Henk Slager.
Kuandu Museum of Fine Arts, Taipei, Taiwan

P. 156, 157, 158, 159
3-D Printed Sculptures
(The Objets Originally from North Korean Film
Worldwide Support for Kim Il Sung), 2018,
Dimensions variable

P. 160
International Friendship, 2018,
3-D Printed Sculptures, books about Ethiopian Communists
and the Relation between Kim Il Sung and African Leaders
installed in the vitrine with two CRT monitors,
140×390×53cm, Kuandu Biennale 2018

CHE Onejoon (b.1979) is a visual artist and filmmaker.

Che studied photography in a vocational high school then started his career as an evidence photographer during military service. One of his first projects involved photographing Seoul's red-light district, which began to decline after the anti-prostitution law took effect in 2004. He also made short films and installations that capture the trauma of modern Korean history by documenting the ruins of the global Cold War: in the form of bunkers constructed in Seoul during the immediate aftermath of the Korean War, and the U.S. Army camps in South Korea vacated when the soldiers redeployed to the Iraq War. In recent years, Che worked on a documentary project about the monuments and statues made by North Korea for many sub-Saharan African nations. His on-going project seeks to create a photographic work, film and installation about Afro-Asian culture and identity. Che has exhibited internationally at the Taipei Biennial (2008), Palais de Tokyo (2012), the Venice Biennale of Architecture (2014), the SeMA Biennale Mediacity Seoul (2014), the New Museum Triennial (2015), the Louisiana Museum of Modern Art (2015), the Busan Biennale (2018), the Latvian Centre for Contemporary Art (2019), Jakarta Biennale (2021), and others. Che was a fellow of Sommerakademie Zentrum Paul Klee 2013 in Bern and Rijksakademie 2017–2018 in Amsterdam.

SOLO EXHIBITIONS (SELECTION)

2021 *Highlife*, The Reference, Seoul, S. Korea
2015 *InFormation*, Sindoh Art Space, Seoul, S. Korea
2011 *Red Cloud*, Ilwoo Space, Seoul, S. Korea
2010 *Paju*, Touchart Gallery, Paju, S. Korea
2009 *Townhouse*, Insa Art Space, Seoul, S. Korea
2008 *Undercooled*, Alternative Space Pool, Seoul, S. Korea
2006 *Underground*, Hyundai Do Art Gallery, Seoul, S. Korea

GROUP EXHIBITIONS (SELECTION)

2021 *Future Tense*, Jim Tompson Art Center, Bangkok, Thailand
2021 Jakarta Biennale, *ESOK*, National Museum of Indonesia, Jakarta, Indonesia
2020 *Who is Gazing?*, Musée du quai Branly, Paris, France
2019 *gohyang: home*, Seoul Museum of Art, Seoul, S. Korea
2019 *Better than Tomorrow*, Main Exhibition, Anyang Public Art Project—*Symbiotic City*, Anyang Pavilion, Anyang, S. Korea
2019 Lubumbashi Biennale, *Future Genealogies, Tales From The Equatorial Line*, Lubumbashi, Congo
2019 SURVIVAL KIT 10.1, Latvian Centre for Contemporary Art, Riga, Latvia
2019 *Civilization: The Way We Live Now*, National Gallery of Victoria, Melbourne, Australia
2018 Kuandu Biennale, *Seven Questions for Asia*, Kuandu Museum of Fine Arts, Taipei, Taiwan
2018 Busan Biennale, *Divided We Stand*, Museum of Contemporary Art Busan, Busan, S. Korea
2018 *Unfixing Histories*, Sign, Groningen, Netherlands
2018 *THE REAL DMZ: Artistic Encounters Through Korea's Demilitarized Zone*, New Art Exchange, Nottingham, UK
2017 *REAL DMZ PROJECT: Aarhus Edition*, Kunsthal Aarhus, Aarhus, Denmark
2017 *RED AFRICA: Things Fall Apart*, Galeria Avenida da Índia, Lisbon, Portugal
2017 *Collective Monument*, Stamp Gallery, University of Maryland, Maryland, USA
2016 *South of the Sahara: Accelerated Urbanism in Africa*, Tel Aviv Museum of Art, Tel Aviv, Israel
2016 *RED AFRICA: Things Fall Apart*, Calvert22, London, UK
2015 *Les Résidences de Photoquai_Cabinet d'art Graphiques*, Musée du quai Branly, Paris
2015 *AFRIKA: Architecture, Culture and Identity*, Louisiana Museum, Humlebæk, Denmark
2015 New Museum Triennale: *Surround Audience*, New Museum, New York, USA
2014 Daegu Photo Biennale, *Photographic Narrative*, Daegu Arts Center, Daegu, S. Korea
2014 SeMA Biennale Mediacity Seoul, *Ghosts, Spies, and Grandmothers*, Seoul Museum of Art, Seoul, S.Korea
2014 *Crow's Eye View: The Korean Peninsula*, Korean Pavilion, Venice Biennale of Architecture, Venice, Italy
2013 Photoquai Biennale, Musée du quai Branly, Paris, France
2013 *The Shadows of the Future*, National Museum of Contemporary Art, Bucharest, Romania
2013 *Photography and Society—Social Art*, Daejeon Museum of Art, Daejeon, S. Korea

2012 *Urban Synesthesia*, ARKI Gallery, Taipei, Taiwan
2012 *Les Modules*, Palais de Tokyo, Paris, France
2012 *Piece pour le Pavillon*, HAU2, Berlin, Germany
2012 *Piece pour le Pavillon*, La Ménagerie de Verre, Paris, France
2012 *Deep Structure*, Yebisu International Festival for Art & Alternative Visions, Tokyo Photographic Art Museum, Tokyo, Japan
2011 *The 11th Hermès Korea Art Prize*, Atelier Hermès, Seoul, S. Korea
2011 *Fashion info Art*, Plateau Samsung Museum of Art, Seoul, S. Korea
2010 *Mouth to Mouth to Mouth*, Salon of the Museum of Contemporary Art Belgrade, Belgrade, Serbia
2010 *Monumental Tour*, Space*C, Coreana Museum of Art, Seoul, S. Korea
2010 *Empty House*, Songwon Art center, Seoul, S. Korea
2009 Gwangju Design Biennale, *The Clue*, Gwangju Biennale Exhibition Hall, Gwangju, S. Korea
2009 *Photo-op*, Photographic Center Northwest, Seattle, USA
2008 *Young Korean Artists*, National Museum of Modern and Contemporary Art, Gwacheon, S. Korea
2008 Taipei Biennial: *Art as Social Discourse*, Taipei Fine Arts Museum, Taipei, Taiwan
2007 *Dual Space: Che Onejoon & Liu Ren*, Gallery Mook, Beijing Dashanzi 798, Beijing, China
2007 *Around Questions of Urbanity*, Canal de Isabel II, Madrid, Spain
2006 *Nine Landscapes of DongSung*, Gallery Jungmiso, Seoul, S. Korea
2005 *Portfolio 2005*, Seoul Museum of Art, Seoul, S. Korea
2005 *K237 Area Improvement Project*, Ssamzie Space, Seoul, S. Korea
2004 *Document*, Seoul Museum of Art, Seoul, S. Korea
2002 Independent Art Festival, Ssamzie Space, Seoul, S. Korea
2001 Independent Art Festival, Ssamzie Space, Seoul, S. Korea

SCREENING
2017 *I'm Monica from Pyongyang*, Art Sonje Center, S. Korea
2016 SBS TV Documentary, *Mansudae Master Class*, S. Korea
2016 *Living on Border*, Silencio by David Lynch, Paris, France
2015 OK. VIDEO FESTIVAL, Galeri Nasional Indonesia, Jakarta, Indonesia
2013 *Spinning Wheel*, 104 Centquatre, Paris, France
2012 International Experimental Film and Video Festival EXiS, Seoul, S. Korea
2012 The 12th International New Media Festival, Hongdae Station, Seoul, S. Korea
2010 International Experimental Film and Video Festival EXiS, Seoul, S. Korea
2010 *The Street and Representing Public Space*, Les Rencontres de la Photographie d'Arles, Arles, France
2007 G+SCREENING, Photography from Korea, INDEXG, Toronto, Canada

PUBLICATION
2009 *Geopolitics of the Visible*, Noonbit Publishing, Seoul, S. Korea

RESIDENCIES
2017 Rijksakademie van Beeldende Kunsten, Amsterdam, Nethelands
2013 Sommerakademie, Zentrum Paul Klee, Bern, Switzerland
2012 Seoul Art Space Geumcheon, Seoul, S. Korea
2011 Palais de Tokyo, Le Pavillon, Paris, France
2011 Samsung Studio, Cite Internationale des Arts, Paris, France
2009 National Art Studio Changdong, Seoul, S. Korea

AWARDS
2012 Artistic Creation Photoquai's Residencies Award, Musée du quai Branly, Paris, France
2011 Finalist of the 11th Hermès Korea Art Prize, Hermès Foundation, Seoul, S.Korea
2010 Ilwoo Photography Prize, Ilwoo Korean airline Foundation, Seoul, S.Korea
2009 Honorable Mention, Photographic Center Northwest, Seattle, USA

Charles K. Armstrong was, until his retirement in July 2020, the Korea Foundation Professor of Korean Studies in the Social Sciences in the Department of History at Columbia University, where he was also the director of the Center for Korean Research. He is the author of several books on modern Korea and East Asia, including *The North Korean Revolution, 1945–1950* (Cornell University Press, 2003), *The Koreas* (Routledge, second edition 2014), and *A History of Modern East Asia, 1800–present* (Wiley-Blackwell, forthcoming 2021). Armstrong holds a B.A. in Chinese Studies from Yale University, an M.A. in International Relations from the London School of Economics, and a Ph.D. in History from the University of Chicago.

Inga Lāce is currently C-MAP Central and Eastern Europe Fellow at MoMA, New York. She has been curator at the Latvian Centre for Contemporary Art since 2012 and was curator, together with Valentinas Klimašauskas, of the Latvian Pavilion at the Venice Biennale 2019 with artist Daiga Grantina. She has also been co-curator of the 7th–10th editions of the contemporary art festival SURVIVAL KIT (with Jonatan Habib Engqvist, 2017, and Angels Miralda and Solvita Krese, 2018–2019, Riga) and has curated exhibitions at the Latvian National Museum of Art, Riga, Villa Vassilieff, Paris, James Gallery at CUNY, New York, Muzeum Sztuki, Łódź, Framer Framed, Amsterdam, de Appel arts centre, Amsterdam, Konsthall C, Stockholm, and Pori Art Museum.

Seon-Ryeong Cho is a researcher, curator, and associate professor at the Department of Art, Culture, and Image at Pusan National University. Her research fields include aesthetics, contemporary art and image / media theory based on psychoanalysis and post-structuralist philosophy. Her books include *Lacan and Art* (2011) and *Image Apparatus Theory* (2018). Cho worked at Busan Museum of Art, Art Space Pool, and Nam June Paik Art Center. Cho has been working as an independent curator since 2010. Her curatorial interests include productive encounters between social and artistic fields and curatorial methodology for video works.

Joanna Lehan is a New York-based educator, editor, writer, and curator focused on contemporary photographic practice. She co-organized numerous large-scale exhibitions at the International Center of Photography between 2003–2017, including three of ICP Triennials. She has contributed essays to exhibition catalogues and monographs, and written about photography for Aperture, Photograph, Time and others. She served as editor of several photography books for Aperture Foundation, including those by Hank Willis Thomas, Trevor Paglen and Thomas Ruff. Presently she teaches writing and contemporary photography in the ICP-Bard MFA program, and at Barnard College.

Chang Joon Ok is a Ph. D. Candidate in the Department of Politics and International Relations at Seoul National University. His research interests are in Cold War history, with a special focus on the global context of Asian / Korean Cold War. His recent publications include *A Contested 'Pacific': Reinterpretation of 1949 Pacific 'Alliance'* (2021), *Contrapuntal Reading on the Writings of Chong-Sik Lee and Bruce Cumings* (2020), *From Korean War Experience to the Psychological Warfare Text* (2017), *The 'Bandung Spirit' in Cold War United States: Third Worldism of Chester Bowles* (2015).

Sun A Moon is a curator, researcher, and writer based in Seoul. She is currently director of Space AfroAsia in Dongducheon. Recent exhibitions and projects include the 6th Anyang Public Art Project—*Symbiotic City*, Anyang Pavilion, Anyang (2019), *Zeitgeist: Video Generation*, Alternative Space Loop, Seoul (2018), *Brace for Impact*, de Appel, Stedelijk Museum, De School, Amsterdam (2018), *Zeitgeist: 非-Psychedelic; Blue*, Amado Art Space, Seoul (2016), *Plastic Myths*, Asian Culture Center, Gwangju (2015–2016). She participated in the TATE Intensive Program in London (2017) and de Appel Curatorial Programme in Amsterdam (2017–2018), and received the Amado Exhibition Award (2016) and the Critic Festival Award (2016).

Sean O'Toole is an author, critic and editor based in Cape Town. He has published two books, *Irma Stern: African in Europe— European in Africa* (2020) and *The Marquis of Mooikloof and Other Stories* (2006), as well as edited three volumes of essays, most recently *The Journey: New Positions on African Photography* (2020). His essays, cultural journalism and reviews have appeared in numerous publications, including *Aperture, Artforum* and *Frieze*. He is a contributing editor to *Frieze* magazine, London, and a founding editor of the urban affairs journal *Cityscapes*. He has written essays for recent monographs by Michael Armitage, Margaret Courtney-Clarke, David Goldblatt, William Kentridge, Jackie Nickerson, Jo Ratcliffe and Mikhael Subotzky, among other artists.

CHE Onejoon
International Friendship: The Gifts from Africa

This publication crystalizes researchs
around Che Onejoon's documentary projects,
International Friendship (2017–2018) and *Mansudae
Master Class* (2013–ongoing).

Published by Kehrer Verlag Heidelberg, 2022
© Che Onejoon and authors

Artworks
Che Onejoon

Texts
Charles K. Armstrong, Che Onejoon,
Seon-Ryeong Cho, Inga Lāce, Joanna Lehan,
Chang Joon Ok, Sean O'Toole

Editor
Sun A Moon (Space AfroAsia)

Translations
Jaewook Lee, Jaeyong Park (Seoul Reading Room)

Copy Editing
Jacco Zwetsloot

Design
Dokho Shin

Image Processing
Kehrer Design (René Henoch)

Production Management
Kehrer Design (Tom Streicher)

This book is published under the support of
Korea Arts Management Service.

Bibliographic information published by the
Deutsche Nationalbibliothek
The Deutsche Nationalbibliothek lists this
publication in the Deutsche Nationalbibliografie;
detailed bibliographic data is available on the
Internet at http://dnb.dnb.de.

Printed and bound in Germany

ISBN 978-3-96900-026-7

Kehrer Verlag Heidelberg
www.kehrerverlag.com

**korea Arts
management
service**

Acknowledgement
The artist would like to thank all the contributors and
participants for the realization of this publication.
He also wishes to acknowledge all the participants and
advisers for *International Friendship* and *Mansudae Master
Class,* and in particular:

Photo Printing
Kyungyul Kim (Image One)

3-D Sculpture
Sungseok Ahn

Miniature Sculpture
Jaehyun Shin

Film Production
Line Producer Sohl Lee (3rd trip)

Assistant Director
Ikhyun Gim (1st trip)
Hakyoung Kim (2nd trip)
Hyunah Kang (4th trip)

Cinematographers
Youngchen Cho, Jongwook Seo
Younghoon Lee (1st Camera)
Changmin Lee (2nd Camera)
Chulmin Jeong (3rd Camera)

Film Editor
Changjae Won (IUM)

Music
Kang Ida, Jeongseob Ahn

This project is supported by
Musée du quai Branly
Institut Français de Kinshasa, RDC
Louisiana Museum of Modern Art
Tina Kim Gallery
The Korean Pavilion, Venice Architecture Biennale 2014
Seoul Foundation for Arts and Culture
Arts Council Korea
Asia Culture Center
Korea Creative Content Agency
Korea Communications Agency

The book cover features

*Statue of Former Vice-President Joshua Nkomo,
rebuilt by Zimbabwean Artist in 2014*
Bulawayo, Zimbabwe, 2015 (Front)
*Site of Demolished Statue of Former Vice-President
Joshua Nkomo, removed in 2011*
Bulawayo, Zimbabwe, 2013 (Back)